Design Revolution

Design Revolution: 100 Products That Empower People

Emily Pilloton
Foreword by Allan Chochinov

Metropolis Books

contents

A Good Long Tradition

Allan Chochinov

From Victor Papanek's *Design for the Real World* to John Thackara's *In the Bubble*, from Buckminster Fuller's World Game to Bruce Mau's Massive Change, there has been a perennial desire to drive home the imperative of design for social good. This appeal can, and has, taken many forms: the well-argued essay, the pissed-off manifesto, the quick-and-dirty practical guide, the sober accounting of best practices. Cameron Sinclair and Kate Stohr's *Design Like You Give a Damn* and Alex Steffen's *Worldchanging* (notice the different tones of their respective titles—not that Alex isn't plenty outraged!) are recent sourcebooks filled with remarkable examples of design for social good (the former with a concentration on architecture, the latter with an emphasis on, well, everything), chronicling projects that attempt to solve critical problems and gesturing toward design solutions that leverage passion and technological foresight.

With its focus on product design, *Design Revolution* enters this group

with a couple of tricks up its sleeve. First, people love stuff. We love objects, artifacts, tools, and gadgets, and we surround ourselves with products—both functional and totemic—as ways to express our identity, structure our days, and prop out our built environments. The power that product design has over us is both astounding and insidious, and our draw to the "new and novel" through media, commerce, and popular culture makes us complicit in the consumerism that plagues our psyches and planet alike. It's not all bad, of course, but it's not all good either.

And as much as people love products, they love systems even more. Wearing a Nike + iPod Sport Kit fitness monitor, for example, might increase the effectiveness of your workout, but the brand experience tethers you to a system of advertising, lifestyle, and tribe-making. (People like that part, by the way.) Joining the Zipcar car-sharing network provides you with on-the-fly access to an automobile, certainly, but it also brings you

membership into a system of like-minded people who together leverage economies of scale, save fossil fuels, and decrease energy and material flows. In fact, when you look at most products in our world, it is difficult to evaluate them in the abstract *without* accounting for their roles in larger systems of interaction, behavior, and culture. This makes the playing field richer, and the dialogue, too; it makes it easier to see hollow wastes of embodied energy (and shelf space) for what they really are, and to admire products that understand and work effectively within their larger contexts.

The second point to make about *Design Revolution* is that it is positively spilling at the guts with displays of ingenuity and resourcefulness. And though many of the devices, products, and services presented in this book are mass-produced, virtually all of them resonate with a kind of hacker's ethos: of doing a lot with a little; challenging the status quo; tinkering with something until it works a little better, or so *much* better that it's transformed into something entirely new. Recently there has been a surge of interest in making—evidenced by an explosion of crafting, hobby, and modding communities, websites, and magazines—and there is something irresistible about using one's hands, coming up with a new idea, and busting it out in three dimensions. Everyone loves to invent something—whether it's a new twist on a cookie recipe or a novel way of attaching a book bag to your bicycle—and when we look at a collection of particularly ingenious inventions like the ones in this book, I believe we feel a unique kind of delight: We are awed, charmed, intrigued...and jealous all at the same time. ("Why didn't I think of that?" is often the highest compliment we can bestow.)

Good Design

There's another appeal to *Design Revolution*: it presents itself as a kind of twist on catalogues of good design. And goodness knows, people (and coffee tables) sure do love a nice catalogue of "good design."

In the art and design section of any bookstore you might find such compilations as *1000 Chairs* (self-explanatory), *Transmaterial* (a collection of new and innovative building materials), even the wacky nonsense gathering in *101 Useless Japanese Inventions: The Art of Chindogu* (a book that tickles our minds on the one hand and shines a spotlight on the madness of our consumer culture on the other).

There are grand collections, too—*Phaidon Design Classics*, a three-volume encyclopedia of 1,000 iconic designs, is the current record-holder at 24 pounds (10.9 kg) and 3,300 pages—but there are more modest efforts that are just as pure in intent. *Humble Masterpieces*, the companion catalogue to Paola Antonelli's 1994 MoMA show of the same name, is a collection of everyday objects, a set of the beloved and the quotidian that we often take for granted precisely because of their ubiquity and unfailing functionality. The creators of these (humble) design icons are sometimes anonymous or go unrecognized, but they've earned their spots in that collection (and in the permanent collection of MoMA!) by grabbing the brass ring of design: they're deemed Good Design. More than the simple marriage of form and function, Good Design manifests an economy of materials, a clarity of purpose, and a delight in use.

And though Good Design has moved from describing Swingline staplers and Braun coffee makers to Apple iPhones and Jawbone NoiseAssassin Bluetooth headsets, the quest for Good Design isn't the only game in town. (You wouldn't use the term to describe the wit centric design gestures of Droog, for instance, or the critical design explorations of Royal College of Art design students.) There's something of a sober, sensible-shoe taint to the term, perhaps, and a removed, abstracted judgment in its application. Nevertheless, if we can accept Good Design as a paragon for the artifacts of design, what can (and should) we expect from the enterprise of design? Is there a distinction between "good design" and "design for good"?

Design for Good

At the start of any worthy design project is a strategic phase—an examination of "exactly what are we trying to do here?" Some practitioners call this needs assessment, some call it problem definition, some call it discovery. But since the best designs always embody their intentions in the final products, what if that intention, from the get-go, is overtly aimed toward some social good? Does that change the kind of product we end up with? (Change the ingredients, change the results; there's that cookie recipe.)

Well, when you are designing something expressly for social good, I'd submit, you've changed the bargain between producer and consumer; you've added elements of social currency that weren't there before. Let's say you set out to design a high-end toaster or an ad campaign for a sitcom, for example. The ingredients are fairly predictable (as are often the results). But if you're trying to get potable water to a community that doesn't have enough to drink, or to design a prosthetic limb for land mine victims, or to make a dent in the epidemic of childhood obesity, the entire equation has changed. Product success or failure can no longer be driven and measured by market forces alone—though many socially progressive designs have floundered by ignoring those rules; there are exogenous criteria that come into play. Here the design conversation moves from form, function, beauty, and ergonomics to accessibility, affordability, sustainability, and social worth. Throw in green materials, renewable energy, cultural appropriateness, responsible labor practices, and a big dollop of respect for the user, and yes, you've got a wholesome recipe for design for social change. One might wish that all designers, all the time, would use this broader set of criteria as they go about designing everything from billboards to buildings, but I believe that designing for good necessitates it.

And this sentence has no doubt been written countless times, but there now seems an urgent mandate to design for good—to understand the practice of design as an unequivocally interconnected, global, and consequence-creating endeavor. I use the word consequence here because designers—be they graphic, product, communication, transportation, or architectural—get up in the morning believing that they are in the artifact business; that they create annual reports or clock radios, exhibition spaces or branding campaigns, and that these artifacts get repeated through print runs of 10,000 or plastic injection molding machines by the millions. But designers would do well to remember that they are not in the artifact business. They are in the consequence business. And for design to truly be a force for positive change, we must always ask what consequences a design creates—from materials and energy use to toxicity, pollution, and social inequality.

So why aren't we seeing a greater rush to design for good? This gets a bit mucky, actually. It is easy to criticize the design profession right now, with its headlong imperative to create supply and demand for all manner of manufactured goods and services. I've previously written that "designers are feeding and feeding this cycle, helping to turn everyone and everything into either a consumer or a consumable," and that when you think about it, this is kind of grotesque.[1] But the enterprise of design—design as a verb—seems to hold in its definition a positive intention. John Thackara, design impresario, founder of Doors of Perception, and global force for good, doesn't believe in the "blame-and-shame" game, in holding designers' feet to the fire. "I've never met a designer who didn't, fundamentally, want to make things better," he argues, and the point is persuasive in the abstract.[2] But it's in the consequences of the actions of all those good-meaning designers that the truth of the design enterprise becomes more visible. Perhaps the wholesale poisonings of every natural system through industrialization are "unintended" consequences, but there's a cruel irony in designers running around, busily creating more and more garbage for our great-grandchildren to dig up, breathe, and ingest, all the while calling themselves "problem solvers." The stakes for design are huge (it's right there in the term "mass production"); so must be its mandates and responsibilities.

And there's another wrinkle here: Some of the best "design solutions" rise forth from people who aren't "credentialed" designers at all. Indeed, many of the designs in this collection are the results of grassroots initiatives, competitions, school assignments, crisis rescue, or ad hoc group efforts. On the broad spectrum, designers can be volunteers, handypersons, tinkerers, and poets. And on the narrow spectrum, the specialization in the maturing field of design right now is extraordinary, rendering the disciplines and jargon between ethnographers, materials technologists, human factors experts, and branding consultants almost exclusionary. The whole notion of what designers are, exactly, seems to become blurrier every year. Alice Rawsthorn, writing recently in the *International Herald Tribune*, ponders: "Then there are all of the areas where design is deployed. Architecture. Engineering. Products. Transport. Fashion. Graphics. Multimedia. Information technology. Social services. Disaster relief, and so on. How can [design] be expected to have a coherent meaning across all of them?"[3]

Good to Go: Solving Problems and Celebrating Life

Well, for me, the enterprise of design distills to at least a couple of things. Sure, design is here to solve problems, but it's also here to celebrate life. And when it comes right down to it, all of those "other" criteria of design for good—the social vectors, the labor vectors, the accessibility, affordability, and empathy vectors—those are precisely the elements that actually do celebrate life; they are the components that have social currency and weight, that respect individuals, communities, and ecosystems appropriately, and contribute to the ennobling potential of design and creative work.

Design Revolution, then, can become a compelling tome for all of us to embrace. Its exuberance, its variety, the varied authorship of its contents—all spilled across these pages points toward something emergent, dynamic, exciting, and, not least, hopeful. If design is enjoying a renaissance in the business press and in the public eye right now, then it is up to designers not only to welcome that new interest but also to leverage it into works of great, positive social change. During the 2008 Summer Olympics in Beijing, a newscaster said of an Olympian that he did one of the hardest things in sports: "winning, when everyone thought you would." I feel that way about design. If a lot of people are expecting design to get

us out of some of the messes we're in right now, then it's up to designers to live up to those expectations and deliver the goods.

In his book *Blessed Unrest*, Paul Hawken argues that we are in the midst of an immense, worldwide movement—for which there is no name, and for which there is no central organization.[4] It's made up of individuals and collectives, decentralized yet unified in mission, who together are creating meaningful change at every level. He likens this movement to a planetary "immune response"— a rising action against the ceaseless assault on the natural and social environment. From people in arts activism and sustainable forestry, to ecolabeling, industrial ecology, pollution remediation, and green banking, Hawken reckons that the movement is over one million strong, spanning fields so diverse that he is attempting to collect them through a website called wiserearth.com (World Index of Social and Environmental Responsibility). This is a hopeful, optimistic

worldview at a time that appears to offer precious few of them, and I cling to this idea, if not as a beacon, then as some kind of affirmation that many, many people—including designers credentialed and not—are out there carrying a torch, making, fighting, and creating design solutions that add value, social worth, and dignity to our world.

I'll carry around *Design Revolution*, then, for within its covers lies a stunningly optimistic set of design initiatives—from far and wide—all aimed directly at the two objectives I hold most dear: solving problems and celebrating life.

1. Allan Chochinov, "1000 Words: A Manifesto for Sustainability in Design," April 2007, http://www.core77.com/reactor/04.07_chochinov.asp.
2. John Thackara, conversation with the author, October 2007.
3. Alice Rawsthorn, "What Defies Defining, but Exists Everywhere?" *International Herald Tribune*, August 17, 2008.
4. Paul Hawken, *Blessed Unrest: How the Largest Movement in the World Came into Being and Why No One Saw It Coming* (New York: Viking, 2007).

Design Can Change the World

Emily Pilloton

An Industrial Design Revolution

I believe that design is problem solving with grace and foresight. I believe that there's always a better way. I believe that design is a human instinct, that people are inherently optimistic, that every man is a designer, and that every problem can either be defined as a design problem or solved with a design solution. And I believe that in an ideal (design) world, there would be no need for this book, because we as designers would be more responsible and socially productive citizens than we have become.

In January 2008, I founded Project H Design based on these ideals with about $1,000 in savings, two design degrees, over $70,000 in student loans, "office space" at the dining room table in my parents' house, and a lot of frustration with the design world. Project H—a nonprofit organization supporting product design initiatives for humanity, habitats, health, and happiness; one part de-sign firm, one part advocacy group—has seen meteoric growth since then. Our global chapters have worked on projects ranging from water transport and filtration systems to educational devices, retail products co-designed with homeless shelter residents, therapeutic solutions for foster care homes, and more. Partner organizations, a committed board of directors and advisors, and hundreds of volunteers have joined our efforts. Most days Project H's "headquarters" is wherever there is Wi-Fi and coffee, and I like to think of our global "coal-ition" as relevant everywhere and based nowhere. As my personal mission has grown into a greater collective drive, Project H has become, I hope, a means to enable designers and to enable life through design. Its growth has both surprised me, given my lack of business acumen, and delighted me, proving that I am not alone in my inability to settle for an in-dustrial design career that does noth-ing but perpetuate the senseless need for, and purchasing of, more stuff.

As a whole, today's world of design (specifically product design) is severely deficient, crippled by consumerism and paralyzed by an unwillingness to financially and ethi-cally prioritize social impact over the bottom line. We need nothing short of an industrial design revolution to shake us from our consumption-for-consumption's-sake momentum. We must elevate "design for the greater good" beyond charity and toward a socially sustainable and economi-cally viable model taught in design schools and executed in design firms, one that defines the ways in which we prototype, relate to clients, distribute, measure, and understand. We must be designers of empowerment and rewrite our own job descriptions. We must design with communities, rather than for clients, and rethink *what* we're designing in the first place, not just *how* we design the same old things. We must constantly find ways to do things better, through both our designs themselves and the ways in which we operate as designers.

On a trip to Cuba in 2000, I became enchanted by the large-scale graphic murals that adorn Havana's concrete surfaces. They read, "En cada barrio, revolución," meaning, "In every neighborhood, revolution." The graphics date to the early 1960s, in the years just following the revolution, when Fidel Castro deployed neighborhood Committees for the Defense of the Revolution (CDRs) to monitor the safety, spending, crime, and counterrevolutionary activity within each community block. Most of the murals, which are gorgeous examples of midcentury graphic design, include the CDR's crestlike symbol, advertising both the omnipresence of "revolution" as an idea and the literal omnipresence of the CDR neighborhood watchmen.

And while the propaganda reeks of a certain "Big Brother" totalitarianism, Cuban citizens tend not to view it that way. The murals' words are still relevant today, as evidenced by new versions of the motto appearing in contemporary graffiti and street art as statements of national identity and individual rights. During my trip, as I stood admiring one of the murals along El Malecón, the often-photographed seaside road in Havana, an elderly man told me, "They are reminders that we can change things. Revolution is in our blood; it's who we are. We'll always fight and try to make our lives better." His description, in many ways, pinpoints both the need and the motivation for this book. Humans have an instinct to seek out better ways, and designers possess the toolbox (and responsibility) to deliver solutions that make those ways accessible and improve life.

As effective designers, we must find efficiencies, bring new function to daily life, and, we hope, do so with some grace or beauty. But our constant search for improvement must extend beyond the things we design to include our own function as designers. Shouldn't being a designer mean more than the traditional model of object maker and creator of more crap? Shouldn't we be trusted to make things better? Shouldn't we be relied upon as problem solvers in times of crisis? I believe that we should and we can, and I hope this book makes the case for the value of such a species of "citizen designers." In this introduction, you will find three sections that define the context ("Ready . . ."), toolbox ("Set . . ."), and actions ("Go . . .") required for a design revolution that puts social impact and human needs first. More than 100 examples in this book's eight categories are evidence of the ability of need-based, humanitarian design to empower and enable individuals, communities, and economies. *Design Revolution* is both a reference and a roadmap, a call to action and a compendium.

The good news is that my personal sentiments are not even remotely uncommon. The tide is turning within design schools, among emerging designers, and in the offices of global design consultancies. Social entrepreneurship has emerged as a business model that effectively supports design for social impact, providing a

sustainable economic framework for the distribution of empowering design solutions. Sharing knowledge through information platforms like the Open Architecture Network and the Designers Accord allows us to more efficiently use and learn from each other's best practices. And global efforts with quantifiable aims, such as the United Nations' Millennium Development Goals, give us something to work toward collectively across disciplines. We have, for perhaps the first time, both the weight of an urgent problem and the power of a collective toolbox to solve some of the biggest global issues. It's a group effort requiring individual commitments. Let's rally the troops: *In every designer, revolution.*

READY...

An understanding of where we've come from, where we are now, and what's at stake

1.01 Precedent and Present

The historical timelines of product design and make-life-better activism deserve their own full-length books, but I would like to highlight a few moments in which these two stories intersect. I believe that design has always been the most direct manifestation of two human instincts: to shape our physical environment and to improve life.

Roman emperor Vespasian built the Colosseum as a means to unite the city though collective entertainment. Henry Ford thought the Model T would provide affordable and accessible mobility to Americans while creating jobs through a new model for industrial-scale production. In the 1930s, under Franklin Delano Roosevelt's Works Progress Administration, large-scale public projects put millions of Americans to work on the construction of some of the best-designed modern marvels, including the Golden Gate Bridge. In 1907, when Dr. Maria Montessori founded the Montessori education program, well-designed, iconic, colorful teaching tools were integral to her curriculum and supported her theory that children learn best through play and engagement with objects (see p. 166 of this book). Modernism, as a school of thought, posited that design could shape a utopian society that would unite and inspire. The precedent for design's ability to improve life is undeniable, and such power is the heart of design, though it is often overlooked or overshadowed by the inertia of consumer-driven forces.

Today the stakes are as high as ever. The need for our build-and-fix instincts to address and heal global social issues is visible and urgent. The United Nations' Millennium Development Goals, which set eight categories of ambitious aims such as "Halve, between 1990 and 2015, the proportion of people who suffer from hunger," have been passionately adopted by many designers as a structured framework for their own practices.[1] At the same time, new models for social entrepreneurship and appropriate technologies are emerging. In short, the bar has been raised for both defining the scope of the problem and developing the capabilities of our toolboxes for solutions. The precedent is present, and the time is now.

1.02 The Problem with Products

Industrial design, the sibling of unjustifiable consumerism, is perpetuated by designers who claim to be trendsetters but are truly slaves to market trends. They have helped create a "googly-eyed" market of constant consumers that Victor Papanek, in his book *Design for the Real World*, calls "our Kleenex culture."[2] While all fields of design are grappling with how to use their problem-solving skills and new business models for social impact, product designers have some scale-specific hurdles. In his "1000 Words: A Manifesto for Sustainability in Design," Allan Chochinov, editor in chief of Core77.com and author of this book's foreword, gets to the heart of the most pressing issue in product design: the blessing and curse of mass production. He observes, "We have to remember that industrial design equals mass production, and that every move, every decision, every curve we specify is *multiplied*—sometimes by the thousands and often by the millions. And that every one of those everys has a price. We think that we're in the artifact business, but we're not; we're in the consequence business."[3] The truth is, product design is about multiplicity that is rooted in the amplification of small ideas, which makes product designers much less contextual and responsive than architects, for example, who usually have specific and singular programs, sites, and clients, and can thus better gauge the path between their actions and subsequent receptions.

Papanek takes this idea a step further, effectively equating product design with a license to kill. (One of the chapters in *Design for the Real World* is titled "Do-It-Yourself Murder: Social and Moral Responsibilities of Design.") He writes, "Before (in the 'good old days'), if a person liked killing people, he had to become a general, purchase a coal mine, or else study nuclear physics. Today, industrial design has put murder on a mass production basis. By designing criminally unsafe automobiles that kill or maim nearly one million people around the world each year, by creating whole new species of permanent garbage to clutter up the landscape, and by choosing materials and processes that pollute the air we breathe, designers have become a dangerous breed. And the skills needed in these activities are carefully taught to young people."[4]

While Papanek represents the militant end of the spectrum, his words, first published in 1970, continue to ring true. (Shouldn't it concern us that his nearly 40-year-old assessment of industrial design is relevant and on-the-money today?) In 2007 toy company Fisher-Price recalled nearly one million toys that had been coated in a lead-based paint. Manufactured in China, the recalled toys included the popular Sesame Street and Dora the Explorer characters. While Fisher-Price (verified by doctors) proclaimed that children were in no immediate danger, prolonged oral contact with the toys could have resulted in significant lead exposure.[5] The seemingly minute decisions made while the products were developed, multiplied by millions, resulted in a truly scary situation for parents worldwide. Product design, as a vehicle and an industry, must own up to its power to both improve and harm on grand scales and use this potential as an opportunity to empower rather than damage, to encourage people-centric engagement, not retail therapy.

1.03 A Misdirected Industry

One of my favorite characters from Pixar's animated film *The Incredibles* is Edna Mode, a designer who makes custom outfits for superheroes and is a self-proclaimed trendsetter (many believe that her character is based on real-life fashion designer Edith Head). "This is a hobo suit, darling," she tells Mr. Incredible of his outdated superhero attire, which she then redesigns. "You can't be seen in this. I won't allow it. Fifteen years ago, maybe, but now? Feh!"[6] Dressed all in black, she's sassy, sharp, self-important (though endearing), and a true caricature of the modern-day designer.

Unfortunately her resemblance to today's actual designers is all too uncanny, and the image of the all-knowing designer in a black (or white) suit endures. Beyond the individual egos of those in the profession, however, the design firm is a mechanism that traditionally caters to corporate clients and their target consumer markets. Generally speaking, design firms and the design world are incestuous and insular. We're obsessed with buzzwords and think tanks, where we should be focused on the user and "do tanks." Many of our so-called "solutions" are effectively designs for design's sake, self-congratulatory artistic exercises that are appreciated primarily within the design community and photographed for design magazines. When these designs are lost on consumers, we ask, "Why?"; the answer is simply because we have failed to make those consumers part of the design equation in any real way. While more design firms are beginning to understand the difference between human and consumer and are making concerted efforts to put humans first, the legacy of design for design's sake still haunts us.

In short, design is in many ways disconnected: from users, from other industries, even from reality. Within the design firm (the primary unit of our industry), we must shed our bad habits and design-centric legacies, create new models for more user-centered processes, and expand both the issues we address and the clients for whom we work. "To make design more relevant is to reconsider what 'design' issues are," explains Bryan Bell in his book *Expanding Architecture: Design as Activism*. "Rejecting the limits we have defined for ourselves, we should instead assume that design can play a positive role in seeking answers to many different kinds of challenges.

We have limited our potential by seeing most major human concerns as unrelated to our work."[7]

1.04 The State of Sustainability

Recent years (let's call this period "Sustainability 1.0") have been characterized by a greater adoption (both in substantive and publicity-inspired ways) of sustainable principles and a disenchantment with the word "sustainable" itself. "Greenwashing"— in which corporations or organizations make claims about environmentally friendly actions that are usually half-hearted attempts done to garner media attention— abounds, while "sustainability" has become something of a sound bite, diluted by its overuse, lack of a solid definition, and irresponsible application. So much so, in fact, that in 2008 Lake Superior State University's annual "List of Words To Be Banished from the Queen's English for Misuse, Overuse, and General Uselessness" was topped off by "green" and "carbon footprint," numbers one and two on the list, respectively. "If I see one more corporation declare itself 'green,' I'm going to start burning tires in my backyard," wrote Ed Hardiman, who nominated the word to be included in the list.[8]

But progress, at least for environmental sustainability, has been made. Corporations have developed comprehensive sustainability reports and strategies, and companies continue to develop green product lines using more efficient methods and choosing healthier materials. Some of the most

substantive solutions have smartly adapted nature's processes and systems for industrial or personal functions. John Todd's Eco-Machines, for example, treat wastewater using the natural cleansing properties of wetland ecosystems (see p. 62). The Air2Water Dolphin 2/dragonfly M18 condenses water vapor from ambient air, filters it, and turns it into potable water, using a natural process as an in-home resource (see p. 50).

Most efforts on the sustainability front, however, have been green-only, that is, focused on environmental footprints and materiality. Sustainability governed by the questions "What's it made from?" and "Is it recyclable?" only goes so far, and somewhere along the way, the human element is lost. Like so many other "movements," environmental sustainability does not exist in a vacuum (we saw this clearly with the fall of modernism): It is only as good as its social understanding and appropriate implementation, and it will falter without public awareness and education. In common usage, "green" and "sustainable" are becoming synonymous, and this is problematic for designers and the world. While "green" means environmentally responsible, "sustainable" encompasses all aspects of responsibility and foresight: environmental, social, economic, cultural, and humanitarian. It's about time we let those last four catch up.

A primary example of the limits of environmental-only sustainability is the recent touting of corn-based polylactic acid (PLA) plastic cups and

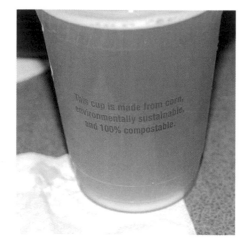

containers. The non-petroleum derived plastic is "compostable and biodegradable" and has been hailed as a greener, healthier alternative to traditional plastics. These new plastic products *are* compostable, but only by a commercial composting standard that requires waste to be heated at a temperature of 140 °F (60 °C) for up to three months. In other words, if you toss the cup in your garden compost pile, it will still be there years from now. Additionally, categorized as number 7 plastic (the catch-all category for plastics that don't fit elsewhere), the items cannot be recycled by any municipal recycling programs. If you were to toss out a corn-based cup with recyclable number 1 or number 2 plastics, its presence could actually be detrimental to the recyclability of the other materials. (Manufacturers recommend the containers be recycled and claim they will decrease distribution if the PLA containers are found to substantially impede existing recycling processes.) And if you were to throw the corn-based items in a trash bin, you could almost guarantee that they would be enclosed in a plastic bag for eternity and thrown in a landfill where the PLA would degrade just as slowly as petroleum-based plastics, requiring an estimated 100 to 1,000 years to decompose entirely.[9] The most troublesome part of the story is that consumers rarely know this; they toss the cups they felt so good about purchasing into the trash, recycling, or compost, where, in all three cases, the material is not performing as advertised. What good is such a "sustainable" product if its proper disposal is neither possible nor understood by users?

The PLA example clearly demonstrates the problems of all "green" products that combine misleading marketing and a lack of consumer education, and it provides us with a departure point from which we can look forward. In the coming years, what are our responsibilities for "Sustainability 2.0?" We must measure progress, share information, hold each other accountable, and bring social sustainability issues up to the same level as the environmental. We're more aware than ever, but we need to put the "human" back in sustainability.

1.05 The Rise of Social Entrepreneurship

While social entrepreneurship is a relatively new business effort, its concept, model, and implementation are complex, and its applications for global well-being are far reaching. There are a few implications, however, that pertain directly to design. Social entrepreneurship, or the social enterprise, in its most basic definition, is the application of entrepreneurial business practices and principles to organize, create, and manage a venture that both incites social change and makes a profit for some or all stakeholders. The goal of social entrepreneurship is to empower individuals, new enterprises, and economies through socially beneficial business ideas. In addition, the bottom line, which traditionally refers only to financial returns, is expanded to what is referred to as the "triple bottom line": people, planet, and profit.

Many give credit for the recent interest in social entrepreneurship to groups like the Acumen Fund, which invests in and manages million-dollar social enterprises across the world, or Ashoka: Innovators for the Public, a global association of the world's leading social entrepreneurs. International Development Enterprises (IDE), a nonprofit organization led by Dr. Paul Polak that helps poor farmers escape poverty, also invests in a business model that empowers the poor to help themselves, supporting new ventures through both design and enterprise. For example, IDE distributes bamboo treadle pumps to increase productivity and profits for small-acreage farmers in Bangladesh and other Asian countries. The pumps are manufactured locally, creating new production enterprises, jobs, and industries, in addition to promoting individual agricultural profits.

For our context, social entrepreneurship is a proven partner in the distribution of design for social impact. Its models, particularly in the developing world, are defined by grassroots entities organized for sustainable profit making and participant empowerment. By adding design to the social entrepreneurship equation, we form a symbiotic relationship between people, product, and profit, bringing design to more socially and fiscally sustainable

arenas, while giving enterprises a tangible and deliverable tool around which to structure production, job creation, and economics.

As an economic model, social entrepreneurship also forces us to look beyond the product itself to what its manufacturing and distribution might enable. Social enterprises value monetary profit as well as human capital, so the success of design through social entrepreneurship is naturally also evaluated on both financial and social metrics. If designers can redefine the success of a product by including its social impact rather than only its profitability, the design process becomes more human centered and user focused.

Design for social impact and social entrepreneurship are, in a sense, made for each other and are so closely intertwined that they are often synonymous. More and more we are seeing design firms use social entrepreneurship models as their means for distribution, while social entrepreneurs are looking to designers to provide the physical solutions to support their business models. The Rockefeller Foundation recently reoriented its organizational priorities toward social entrepreneurship as a new model for philanthropy. In 2008 it provided substantial funding to IDEO for the development of a workbook for design firms. The workbook provides a step-by-step outline of strategies for designing for social impact within firms.[10]

Within this design approach, there's much talk of the "bottom of the

IDE's bamboo treadle pump in use in India

pyramid" or the "other 90 percent," a reference to Polak's statement, "The majority of the world's designers focus all their efforts on developing products and services exclusively for the richest 10 percent of the world's customers. Nothing less than a revolution in design is needed to reach the other 90 percent."[11] While there are some divisive "us-versus-them" connotations inherent in the 10-percent/90-percent approach (see section 3.11), the statement is a reminder to the design world to expand what we consider "design problems" beyond consumer trends and toward real human needs. Social entrepreneurship is a tool with which to make this transition in a more meaningful, economically viable way for users as well as the design industry.

1.06 The World Is Flat-ish

Thomas L. Friedman, author of *The World Is Flat*, argues that in our era of globalization more people than ever before have more access to a horizontally integrated world: one where technology is the means by which individuals have more equal opportunities to compete and succeed. The world is flat, he says, but not necessarily equal, as not everyone has access to this "flat platform."[12] With technology constantly advancing, what is our collective responsibility as designers to apply these developments to provide more people with access to Friedman's flat platform of competition and success? Just because you have the ability to send digital files to a friend across the room via Blue-tooth, does that necessarily mean the same technologies should be implemented in the developing world? Is it inappropriate or even arrogant for us to "force" them on other cultures? Are we doing a service or a disservice? The application and dissemination of technology is a battle of values, requiring foresight, constant user feedback, and, most important, an understanding of social, economic, and cultural contexts. It cannot, however, be separated from a conversation about design for social impact. We must understand the power of technology and act accordingly as designers who wish to serve the underserved.

The term "leapfrogging" refers to a theory that says developing markets should be able to skip, or leap over, inferior or less efficient technologies and move directly to the more advanced ones. The cell phone is the perfect example: Developing countries did not need to first use the telephone, then cordless models, then go through iterations of clunky car phones to arrive at today's cell phone. In a short period of time, many nations transformed from areas with virtually no phone infrastructure to places where the cell phone is nearly ubiquitous.

The aim of leapfrogging is to promote greater access to resources to enable productivity and economic growth. However, the theory has been criticized for its lack of social integration and basis in "forced" technology. Its success is unpredictable, too, as different technologies are accepted in different ways in different cultural contexts. "Developmental histories do not all follow the same path," observes Jamais Cascio, co-founder of online journal *Worldchanging*. "Technologies and ideas which seem somewhat powerful when implemented in the West may be utterly transformative in locations not laden down with legacies of past development. The future belongs to those best able to change along with it; sometimes, starting from nothing can be an engine for just that sort of change."[13]

One of the primary critiques of the One Laptop Per Child XO computer is that its aesthetic and technology have leapfrogged the more basic needs of some of the developing world demographics for which it is intended, diminishing its impact for some users (see p. 172). On a recent trip to Uganda, I showed a photograph of the laptop to an elementary school teacher, to which he replied, "What is that thing?" When I explained that it was a laptop designed for children and intended to facilitate in-class networked learning experiences, he responded, "Most of our students have never even seen a computer." Finally, when I explained some of the product capabilities, his eyes remained fixed on the picture, before replying, "That would get broken in five minutes. Who's going to fix it? Our teachers don't know computers." However, based on enthusiastic feedback from students, teachers and administrators, some northern California schools, for example, have expressed great interest in implementing the laptops as part of an interactive curriculum. These different responses to the computer are not shortcomings of the product; they demonstrate the importance of using technologies appropriately and serve as a reminder that no technology is universally effective.

Alternatively, India's Freedom HIV/AIDS games demonstrate the success of an innovative interface applied to a ubiquitous technological platform in the developing world: the cell phone (see p. 94). Created as a social initiative by ZMQ Software Systems, the four games teach about HIV/AIDS prevention and are downloadable for free from Indian mobile phone service providers. In this case, the games use the existing widespread infrastructure of the cell phone to leverage the implementation of a public health agenda. The public's acceptance of the games demonstrates that the issue is not whether innovative technologies should be promoted in places that lack access to them, but how to do so appropriately (see section 3.09 for more on appropriate technologies). Without contextual understanding and user feedback, a design for social impact will likely fall short of its intentions—however good they are.

SET . . .

An inventory of our toolbox, new frameworks, and models

2.01 Design and Citizenship

In 2008 I visited San Francisco–based fuseproject and spoke to founder Yves Behar about his work on the newly launched NYC Condom Campaign, a project he described as "civic design" (see p. 104). The word "civic" struck me as a perfect descriptor for what design should be, since it refers to society and citizenship, the collective and the individual.

Steven Heller aligns citizenship and design in his book *Citizen Designer: Perspectives on Design Responsibility*. He argues that for design to be a force for the betterment of society, it is paramount that the designer identify himself as a citizen. Heller opens his introduction to the book: "Milton Glaser often says, 'Good design is good citizenship.' But does this mean making good design is an indispensable obligation to the society and culture in which designers are citizens? Or does it suggest that design has inherent properties that when applied in a responsible manner contribute to a well-being that enhances everyone's life as a citizen?"[14] I believe both provocations are true: that design for societal benefit is a personal obligation, and that design can, in fact, make life better. A citizen designer, then, is one who is able to balance the two. A citizen designer must also be responsible, and willing to be held accountable, for his actions and their

reactions. If you want to solve real problems, you must be willing to take on the real consequences. If you're designing water filters, you must take responsibility if the filter does not effectively remove E. coli and then take measured action to fix your mistake. Heller concludes his introduction with a reference to responsibility as a key element of a designer's character: "To be what . . . we call a 'citizen designer' requires more than talent. As Glaser notes, the key is to ask questions, for the answers will result in responsible decisions. Without responsibility, talent is too easily wasted on waste."[15]

2.02 The Untrained Designer as Expert

One of the simplest, most functional rainwater catchment systems (see p. 76) I have come across consisted of a jerrican and a rolled banana leaf, fashioned outside of a guest house in southern Uganda. More citizens worldwide are taking solution making into their own hands. Between the marketability of DIY projects for personal devices and grassroots enterprises in the developing world, the designer is only one player at the problem-solving round table. This is not to say that our trade is becoming obsolete; rather, that we have more collaborators, a broader skill set, and a wider scope. The untrained designer—whether a professional from another field, a farmer in rural Africa, or even a child—has become more than a client or user, now serving as a co-designer and expert on her own environment. With more parties

as co-designers and experts, we can design *with* communities, rather than *for* clients. As this individual initiative to make things work in new ways becomes more commonplace, our solutions as designers must cater to, and learn from, that movement. We must be better listeners and collaborators, learning from the tinkerings and expertise of unexpected partners and enabling clients and users to employ our solutions as platforms from which to invent and adapt beyond the immediate functions of the products.

Maya Pedal, a project based in Guatemala, does just this: Its "bicycle machines" transform bike parts into industrial and agricultural tools (see p. 290). The plans for the machines, which range from blenders to grain grinders, are open source, and the devices are built with local materials by local workers. While none of Maya Pedal's "bikesmiths" are trained designers, their solutions are thoughtful, systemic, beautiful, and appropriate. In adapting the tools to their needs and skills, the individuals and groups, in essence, become designers of systems for ongoing productivity and efficiency.

In a 2001 interview for the journal *inForm*, architect Stanley Tigerman pointed out the difference between the words "professional" and "amateur." "'Pro'-fession' means that you're doing it for a return: If you're a professional athlete, you get paid," he explained. "The etymology of the word 'amateur,' where you do something for love, is better."[16] If we are defining design as "problem solving with grace and foresight," you'll find that designers, or those who employ such creative problem solving, exist in every corner of the world, using context, material, and ingenuity to produce systems that work. Creations from untrained designers can often shed the most light on what a functional and user-accepted solution to a real problem actually looks like. What this means for us as designers is not only that we have more partners and stories to hear, but also that we can work to empower more citizens to become designers in their own lives.

2.03 Design (Thinking) as Business Asset

The term "design thinking" has taken root recently, referring to the use of design sensibilities in business strategies and innovation models. Tim Brown, CEO of IDEO, is often credited with the development and encouragement of design thinking. The idea is nondisciplinary, looking to a designer's mindset as a framework for understanding and creating innovative business propositions. In 2005 Brown laid out a five-step plan for how businesses can apply design thinking to their enterprises. The steps are: hit the streets, recruit T-shaped people (people with both broad knowledge and a particular expertise), build to think, the prototype tells a story, and design is never done.[17] Brown claims these principles have not only applications but also quantifiable economic results for businesses. "It all comes back to the fact that in order to really raise innovation productivity within

NYC Free
Condom dispenser
by fuseproject

organizations, at the strategic level and everywhere else, you have to increase the amount of design thinking inside organizations. Doing so helps you get to clarity faster, helps your organization understand where you're taking it, helps you figure out whether you're on the right track, and enables you to adapt quickly to change. Those are pretty valuable survival skills."[18] For example, when the City of Denver sought to provide solutions to its homeless problem, its approach was one of design thinking rather than turning to legislation or bureaucratic methods. In partnership with nonprofit Denver's Road Home, which advocates for the end of local homelessness, the city hit the streets with the Donation Meter Program, an initiative that reused parking meters to collect donations to be put toward city education and shelter programs for the homeless (see p. 278). Research had revealed that citizens were giving to homeless individuals on the street, but that money was often going directly to drug or alcohol purchases.

The city's program took advantage of the existing donation habit but put it to better use. In combination with a common object (the parking meter) and a well-branded presentation, the city raised $2,000 in the program's first month, with a goal of $100,000 in the first year. In this case, creative thinking and research brought a viable design solution to a civic cause.

Design thinking is not only a business asset, but also a strategy by which designers can find more support from external disciplines. As this approach becomes more deeply ingrained outside of design firms, we will have more natural partners and collaborators working toward the same goals for social impact. An entire section in this book, Enterprise, is dedicated to such initiatives (see pp. 272–99).

2.04 Design as Activism
Victor Papanek's *Design for the Real World* was arguably the first text to militantly and unapologetically push for the reorientation of the design industry toward activism and humanitarian values. But design as activism is really nothing new: Design and the shaping of our physical world are inherently social statements and forces for change. As a frame of mind, design as activism is optimistic and action-based. When design is activism, design is a verb.

The difference today is that the business world is running parallel to the activism of design, finding new ways to equate social and financial values, which brings viability to design activism. Social entrepreneurship models and a more inclusive design process deliver new players to the table and make the funding structure more complex yet far reaching. Technology and information-sharing support the implementation and dissemination of great ideas in more places. The Internet, open-source design, and cell phones (particularly in the developing world) can make more design solutions available to more people, increasing the audience and scope of design activism.

Publicolor students participate in after-school Paint Club program

At the same time, as with most activist movements, people are mobilizing. Organizations and coalitions from Architecture for Humanity and Design Corps to the Designers Accord and Project H (shameless plug for my own nonprofit) are bringing communities together. Larger entities including the United Nations, the American Institute of Graphic Arts, and academic institutions are forming internal groups to better understand design thinking and use it to improve their organizations and lives around the world. Couple all this with the imperatives of global warming, worldwide hunger, and threats to water sanitation and health, and we're at a moment in which the needs are neck-and-neck with the tools for success. We know what is at stake, and we have (or are inventing) the tools with which we can make change.

2.05 Design as Catalyst

In chemistry a catalyst is a substance that increases the rate of a chemical reaction. In essence it makes things happen and makes them happen faster. However, it is also a multiplier and a renewable resource. In the process of catalysis, the catalyst is not consumed; it can participate in multiple chemical transformations. This process, as an analogy, makes sense for design and brings a new perspective to its role as a catalyst. Design can be a catalyst for individual users, communities, even economies, and we, as designers, can serve as catalysts to bring additional value to that which already exists. Design must not just inspire action and reaction; it must amplify impact. It must also be iterative for multiple scalable applications, so it can be used repeatedly as a resource for change.

If we delve even more deeply into the analogy, we discover that catalysts are often favored by chemists because, when introduced, they create chemical transformations that result in very little waste. Similarly, we must look to design as a transformation without waste, one that optimizes the tools and materials at-hand to change situations in efficient and purposeful ways. At the end of the chemistry experiment, we see that the products of a catalytic reaction are often more stable and economically viable substances than were the elements in the initial composition. The production of biodiesel, for example, relies on both inorganic and biocatalysts, resulting in a viable fuel that is more stable than its ingredients or catalysts alone. So, too, must design serve as a strengthener, rather than a force that creates change for the sake of change.

Using design as a catalyst means utilizing design processes or principles to inspire something greater. For example, New York City–based Publicolor works with students to repaint their schools to bring new life to the inner-city institutions (see p. 294). The nonprofit employs paint and graphic design to increase academic engagement and, eventually, graduation rates. Through the painting, Publicolor schools become more welcoming and productive environments, while coordinated after-

school programs improve grades and academic achievement. In the case of Publicolor, design, color, and paint are the catalysts for the social impacts of improved education and achievement for underperforming public schools and students.

2.06 Design as Civics

Design can be a political tactic for city-, country-, and worldwide civic benefit. While there is no federal "Department of Design," there are

certainly precedents, in the USA and abroad, for using design solutions as a means to provide resources, capital, services, and programs to citizens. The free condom campaign designed by fuseproject was a New York City Department of Health and Mental Hygiene initiative, for example. Design can facilitate the effective broadcasting and integration of public programs and can also be a vehicle to incite political change.

After Hurricane Katrina, hoards

of designers and organizations poured into New Orleans and the Gulf Coast region, offering aid in the form of cash, goods, and design services. Architecture for Humanity's Biloxi Model Homes program brought quality architecture to a devastated community and went beyond providing shelter to propose better building standards (both structurally and aesthetically) amid the bureaucratic turmoil of the rebuilding process. In New Orleans, Architecture for Humanity fellow John Dwyer designed and engineered a replicable house foundation to withstand future storms, and he supplemented the foundation with a "kit of parts" that made it possible for architects to quickly and efficiently design durable, affordable homes for residents. The process resulted in the design of more than 60 homes in six months for displaced citizens of the Lower Ninth Ward. In these cases, design was more than the solution; it was a proposal for the government to match the standards set by designers, effectively revealing what a feeble effort the FEMA trailer was and proving the case for design as healing process. The successes of these initiatives demonstrate the strength of design as civics. For it to grow and continue to create change around the world, civic design must come from both top-down and bottom-up initiatives. Political and government entities must employ design thinking to engage citizens, and citizens must bring design thinking to political situations in an effort to provide grassroots solutions.

2.07 Design as Public Health

In 1992 controversial British artist Damien Hirst unveiled his *Pharmacy* at the Cohen Gallery in New York. The room-sized installation consisted of shelf after shelf stocked with prescription pill bottles. The large scale of the shelves and the sheer number of bottles forced the viewer to immediately engage with the work. When asked to describe his inspiration, Hirst said, "I like the way art works, the way it brightens people's lives up . . . but I was having difficulty convincing the people around me that it was worth believing in. And then I noticed that they were believing in medicine in exactly the same way I wanted them to believe in art."[19]

Why do we not feel the same way about design? Why do we not trust design as something that heals us, something we can rely on to make our lives better? While art is merely statement, design is statement, action, and solution, making it a much more viable candidate for trust and belief, the same way medicine is. Target's redesigned prescription bottle provides a literal example, making personal health more accessible through straightforward, beautiful, and well-organized design (see p. 94). Design can heal, be prescribed as a solution, and, more literally, promote health for individuals and larger demographics.

From an industry perspective, we would do well to align the design process with a public health model, one that is based on a broad understanding of demographics, delivery of programs and services for basic human needs, engagement in constant research, and qualitative and quantitative measurement of results. Writing about architecture in his foreword to Bryan Bell's book *Expanding Architecture: Design as Activism*, Thomas Fisher, dean of the College of Design at the University of Minnesota, states, "A public health model for design practice would be good not only for

One of John Dwyer's post-Katrina houses in New Orleans

the many people served by it but also for the architectural profession itself, which has long suffered from a dearth of data to demonstrate the value of what we do."[20]

Public health is usually closely tied to local, state, and national health systems, giving it the civic infrastructure and institutional support needed for broader social impact. Public health professionals also tend to look to prevention over Band-Aid fixes (you'll notice that the NYC Condom Campaign promotes the prevention, not treatment, of HIV/AIDS, sexually transmitted diseases, and unexpected pregnancy). Retail therapy, ironically, is an example of design "healing" in all the wrong ways. We *shop* to make us feel better? The intention, however, is promising: If more objects can bring us comfort, we must reorient public priorities to value design solutions that physically, emotionally, or economically heal us in more substantive ways without perpetuating consumer habits.

2.08 Design as Capital

While I'd hate to say it's all about the money, for many, it is. Designing for underserved demographics often means, first and foremost, providing a way for the people within those groups to make money or, more precisely, to make money as capital to leverage into continued and sustainable income. Using a small amount of capital to propel oneself into a steady income and create a self-supporting business is the concept behind, and the subsequent success of, the

microloan. Online community Kiva allows you to lend a small amount of money to a specific entrepreneur in the developing world. The organization reported a loan repayment rate of 96.89 percent (as of December 2008), and has funded thousands of new, small enterprises worldwide.[21] Grameen Bank, founded by 2006 Nobel Peace Prize winner Muhammad Yunus, has dispersed over $7.43 billion in microloans at a repayment rate of 98.24 percent (for Yunus's work with Grameen Danone, see p. 286).[22] Evidence inarguably demonstrates that poor citizens participating in microfinance programs are able to increase their incomes and improve well-being significantly more easily than those who do not.

Design can play a similar role. By replacing a check with design— a tool for productivity and income generation—the result is more than blanket financial capital; it is a device with specific and immediate functionality for a particular trade or industry. The MoneyMaker deep irrigation water pumps, designed by nonprofit KickStart in collaboration with IDEO, provide an example of design as capital with quantifiable economic results. "Handouts will not solve poverty," KickStart proclaims.[23] Its range of agricultural water pumps increases irrigation capacity for small-acreage farmers in the dry season, providing steady income and increased productivity year-round. Beyond the immediate functionality of the pumps, their production, distribution, and implementation have resulted in 70,769

new enterprises and $77 million in profits and revenue generated annually (as of August 2008).[24] In place of a microloan, the MoneyMaker pump can provide non-financial capital, enabling an agricultural worker and landowner to immediately transform his business into a more sustainable entity for his family and community, since he can hire more workers, buy more land, and grow and sell more of his product.

The parallel between capital and design is based on the provision of a resource for personal economic gain and ongoing self-sufficiency. Rather than viewing design as a material, we should see design as a form of capital that empowers.

GO...

Actionable tactics to start a design revolution for social impact

3.01 Step Up

Now is the time to act. One of my unofficial mantras is "Just do some-thing." It's a reminder to myself, Project H designers, and others that the power of productivity is our greatest asset, that movement and action are our greatest resources, and that socially productive design can be an individual and immediate priority. Given the context and toolbox, how should we proceed with responsibility and foresight? Is there a roadmap toward viable design solutions for social impact? A recipe for best practices for product designers who give a damn?[25] Perhaps design is too complex a process to codify directions for designing well and doing good. But like many a business deal, it can start with a handshake: a simple personal commitment to subscribe to a collective set of ethics that guide us individually and as an industry. Just as medical graduates take the Hippocratic Oath to define a code of conduct, we too need such a commitment.

Oaths and ethical codes exist for many industries and groups beyond doctors, from lawyers to collegiate sports teams, the Boy Scouts of America, and even hackers (who have as guiding principles A Hacker's Code of Ethics). Particular to product design, however, our responsibility and accountability must be equally robust because our actions have personal, social, and physical ramifications for humans and the environment on large scales. We must uphold an ethical standard that both unites us collectively and is adoptable and executable individually. Beyond responsibility, we have a duty to be at the forefront of both social entrepreneurship and constant ingenuity, using our skills to do good and improve life.

What follows, The Designer's Handshake, is a code of conduct for designers, particularly industrial designers, who want to work in more responsible ways. It outlines the core values to which all "citizen designers" should subscribe, but leaves room for personal addenda and further articulation. These are not tactics (which are outlined in the rest of this essay), but values and principles to guide action. The Designer's Handshake serves as a

blueprint for individual direction and a punch-list for collective progress.

It's time to stop talking and start walking. Or even better, let's be co-ordinated and savvy enough to walk and talk at the same time. If you want to commit to ethical, socially meaningful, sustainable design practices and values, sign The Designer's Handshake for your own records, and if you're feeling inspired, send me a copy with your feedback and addenda.

3.02 Human-Centered Sustainability: What, Not Just How

In his introduction to *Design Like You Give a Damn*, Cameron Sinclair states, "We have demonstrated, and hope to continue to do so, that for every 'celebrity architect' there are hundreds of designers around the world, working under the ideal that it is not just how we build but what we build that matters."[26] This "what vs. how" distinction pinpoints both the problem with sustainability as we know it and what the solution might be. Most sustainable design efforts to date have focused on what things are made of, how they are made, what their lifecycles are, and how we as designers bring them to life—in other words, HOW we design. But few of these efforts go back to square one to consider if what we're producing is even valuable to society in the first place—the WHAT of it. Human-focused sustainability requires a re-examination of what we're designing in the first place. Is that $500 vase made from recycled glass more sustainable than a tool for HIV/AIDS

education simply because of how it was made? We must reprioritize the objects that make up our product world to value the things that heal and empower and redefine sustainability based on what we're producing in the first place, rather than simply the means by which those things are made. We must evaluate the "what," and only then use responsible "how" decisions to bring those ideas to fruition.

The reasons for the environmental-over-social hierarchy discussed in section 1.04 are many: You could argue that progress within environmental efforts is more easily measured and advertised and certainly more immediately profitable. The qualitative and subjective nature of the human element of sustainability is a much more complex standard to define and uphold. But sustainability is not simply about what things are made of, but how they improve life and empower people now and for generations to come. Let us put environmental sustainability not on the back burner but on a side burner, giving social sustainability equal weight.

We can do this using two frameworks. The first is designing systems that are sustainable in material yet can also be implemented and understood by their users. This requires a thorough understanding of our users, based on fieldwork and new strategies for human-centered research. We do not want to lose the environmental value. Second, we must approach both environmental and social sustainability as inevitably insepa-

The Designer's Handshake

I, ... ,

as an individual engaged within a greater design community, promise to try, to the best of my ability, to commit and adhere to the following principles within my work and life as a designer:

To go beyond doing no harm:
I will engage only in design activities that improve life, both environmental and human. I will recognize that design that does not improve life is a form of apathy and that "doing no harm" is not enough. I will engage only in design processes that are respectful, generative, catalytic, and productive.

To listen, learn, and understand:
I recognize that every client, partner, or stranger is someone to learn from. I will listen before assuming. I will seek to understand the historical, geographical, social, cultural, and economic context and precedents before beginning the design process.

To measure, share, and teach:
I will measure results quantitatively and qualitatively. I will, as appropriate, make my best practices, successes, tools, and failures available to colleagues for community-based learning.

To empower, heal, and catalyze:
I will use design as a tool to empower people, to make life better, to bring health and improve life, and to enable users to help themselves. I will seek out systemic solutions over quick fixes.

To be optimistic but critical:
I will employ perpetual optimism as a design and business strategy but will apply the same critical evaluation toward social and humanitarian design work that I would any other product. Just because it's "for the greater good" doesn't make it good design.

To think big and have no fear:
I will take calculated risks and not be afraid to use design as a tool for change. I will explore new models for how design can have the greatest impact for the greatest number.

To serve the underserved:
I will look first to demographics underserved by design and propose viable solutions for such groups as the homeless, the sick, the ailing, the young and old, the handicapped, poor, and incapacitated.

To not reinvent the wheel:
When something works well, I will not assume I can or should start from scratch. I will use what it is available to me and look to local resources, skill sets, and materials.

To not do what I don't know:
I will acknowledge the limits of my expertise and will not hesitate to say "no" or to pass projects to another designer who may do a better job.

To always put the user first:
I will always place need over consumption and the human being over the market. I will consider human value, experience, and consequence above all else.

To do good business with good people:
I will be honorable in business and partnerships. I will build distribution into my design, and employ businesses that maximize social impact. I will align myself and work with individuals and groups who have the same values as I do.

To own up and repair:
I will take responsibility for any failures or mistakes I may make and take measures to repair and understand my errors.

To be part of a greater whole:
I will remember that I am a part of a system and a community of designers, users, clients, and global citizens. I will recognize that my individual decisions affect this greater group, and that I have a responsibility to contribute productively.

Insert personal addenda here:

....

....

....

....

signed:

....

date:

....

e-mail address:

....

Please mail copy to:
**Project H Design
PO Box 12021
San Rafael, CA 94912**

rable and complementary entities. Many argue that we as humans have been the sole contributors to nearly all of the planet's ailments, and we therefore have the responsibility to heal both the planet and ourselves. As we are part of the ecosystems we have destroyed, we cannot view the human-environmental sustainability continuum as two-sided; it is a single entity. Environmental and social sustainability are, in fact, based on the same central tenet: the support, health, and empowerment of our world, both human and natural.

Above all, let us step back to consider whether the objects we as designers are giving life to are worth adding to our physical worlds in the first place. Are they merely accessories or are they tools that empower? In essence, give due attention to the what, not just the how, the social, not just the environmental.

3.03 Small Steps and Big Plans
"Elisha Otis did not invent the elevator," said Valerie Casey in a lecture in January 2008.[27] Casey, creator of the Designers Accord, "a Kyoto Protocol for design," went on to explain that though many attribute the invention of the modern elevator to Otis, he, in fact, created the safety catch that prevented the cage from plummeting to the ground. The elevator had been in use as a vertical transport device for nearly 5,000 years when, in 1853, Otis unveiled his invention at the World's Fair in New York. While he did not invent the elevator, Otis is usually credited with it because his incremental improvement added value to a pre-existing system, changing the use of that system forever. This improvement facilitated the modern elevator and, ultimately, the growth of skyscrapers and urban landscapes worldwide.[28]

The example brings to light what Casey refers to as "the designer's dilemma—the tension that exists in the space between inventing and improving."[29] How good is good enough? How much innovation constitutes invention? Is just improving enough? The answer, it seems, is that incremental design is a natural, viable process for widespread innovation, but those small increments must be part of a broader plan driven by a thoroughly articulated goal.

This has become evident in recent years with the advent of the "Age of Sustainability," or Sustainability 1.0, which some would argue quickly turned into the "Age of Greenwashing." The difference between half-hearted versus effective incremental progress can be seen by comparing two examples: John Mayer and Wal-Mart. In 2007 singer and songwriter John Mayer announced his campaign for environmental sustainability, which he dubbed "Light Green." The premise of the campaign was that average people do not want to change their entire lives to go green. Mayer proclaimed, "No thinking about 'offsetting your carbon footprint.' No rallies. No browbeating people who think the Earth just has a fever. Pick one thing to change this year, and keep the rest of your life the same."[30]

Mayer's argument is the equiva-

Patent drawing for Elisha Otis's elevator braking system

lent of saying that half a loaf of bread is better than nothing, but really, the Light Green campaign only dilutes the responsibility individuals have to do their part. It effectively says, "Do one thing and call it a day." What it does not say is, "Do one thing, then next year do two." And what it definitely does not say is, "Do one thing, then next year do two. Here is why you should, and here is how it will improve your own life."

Compare this effort to Wal-Mart, which in late 2006 declared it would start selling compact fluorescent lightbulbs (CFLs) and, in 2007, would sell 100 million of them.[31] Many wondered how big a step the promotion of green lightbulbs really was for a company plagued by criticism for its track record of questionable treatment of employees and wiping small businesses off the map. But Wal-Mart was prepared, also announcing a larger, more holistic corporate sustainability plan that used the retail giant's power for good, effectively forcing companies that made products ranging from laundry detergents to food products to rethink packaging and cut back on waste.[32] Of course, Wal-Mart is not perfect, but its 100 million CFL campaign, while small, mattered because it was one step of many toward corporate environmental, social, and organizational responsibility.

3.04 Taking the Product Out of Product Design

Fred Cuny, a disaster relief specialist who was active from the 1970s through the 1990s (fondly known as "the man who tried to save the world"), was in many ways the pioneer of applying design thinking without material, a product designer without a product.[33] During the Great Ethiopian Famine in the mid-1980s, Ethiopians fled to Sudan in the hopes of finding more reliable food supplies. Cuny traveled to the refugee camps to provide assistance. His immediate response was an aversion to the arrangement of the refugee tents, which were laid out in a traditional grid. Cuny believed a concentric-circle plan would foster social coherence, decrease criminal activity within the camp, and encourage community resource pooling. While the famine remained his priority, he thought this design solution would build more secure communities and hence a stronger foundation for the delivery and receipt of aid. As predicted, the reorientation of the camp based on Cuny's plan was an immediate improvement for inhabitants, reducing crime, increasing trust, and creating microcommunities that supported each other and shared resources.[34] The change required no materials or cost, simply a reexamination of an existing system. While no one called Cuny a designer, his simple solution for efficiency is a perfect example of design thinking and design solutions without material.

Tony Flynn, a material scientist and ceramics lecturer from The Australian National University who developed a simple recipe for making water filters from clay, coffee grounds, and cow manure, is also not dubbed a designer (see p. 58). His solution to nonpotable water was effectively a set of instructions for a DIY filter, though the approach and method behind its development was without a doubt a design process.

Many product design firms have expanded their offerings to include service design, a process during which they look at a client's operational, business, or marketing needs and suggest new models and strategies to reach customers. Service design may be the new "objectless" product design, employing similar creative thinking but resulting in a deliverable based on human factors rather than matter.

As designers, we must challenge ourselves to think about what a solution looks like without the material. What does impact look like? Can we redefine product design so it's not dependent upon products? Is there a way to deliver an efficient and sustainable solution without relying on the production of a highly engineered, virgin object? Design thinking should be a solution-building process rather than something to be approached with an object-as-solution mindset. Some solutions require nothing but problem solving and the identification of opportunities for improved efficiency.

3.05 Impact Over Function

As product designers, we're trained to design things that work and things that are beautiful. But both function and beauty are short-term: A beautiful object may incite a visceral reaction that causes a consumer to purchase it, while its function delivers an immediate service or usability. All products have a finite shelf life, which is defined both by the user and by the function as created by the designer. Impact, on the other hand, is a longer-term goal. To design for impact means looking beyond how something works to what it enables the user to do.

When D-Lab at the Massachusetts Institute of Technology (MIT) designed and engineered sugarcane charcoal in Haiti, the immediate function was to provide a cleaner-burning fuel for cooking (see p. 146). But the charcoal's impact is far greater than its provision of a healthier cooking process. Haiti is 97 percent deforested, which means that charcoal from an agricultural by-product preserves the few remaining trees while the process makes use of a waste material and teaches valuable fuel production skills to local communities.[35]

Frederick Law Olmsted, famed landscape designer and one of the men behind New York's Central Park, designed and built between the 1850s and the 1870s, understood the value of thinking long term. In a letter to his son, Frederick Jr., after the completion of the park, he wrote, "I have all my life been considering distant effects and always sacrificing immediate success and applause to that of the future. In laying out Central Park we determined to think of no result to be realized in less than 40 years."[36] Olmsted inherently understood the value of impact. For us, the mental shift to think beyond an object's immediate use may or may not directly

Tony Flynn makes clay water filters in a cow dung fire

influence the design of the object itself, but the reorientation of the design process will certainly prioritize the design of tools to create generative and longer-living products.

3.06 Innovation for Ingenuity
While attending a business innovation conference in 2008, I sat quietly in the back, tallying. In just two days, presenters and speakers had collectively uttered the word "innovation" (or "innovate" or "innovative") 156 times. One speaker, an executive of a big-box electronics company, even used the word to describe his stores' checkout experience. I thought, *"Really?"* as I added number 157. The truth is, innovation has become something of a buzzword. But the word is not without merit; it simply needs some definition.

Innovation is traditionally tied to the business of design and often involves new technologies. We talk about the iPhone and the newest Dyson vacuum cleaner as "feats of innovation," but we would hesitate to call a DIY water filter in rural Africa innovative. We often equate the new with the innovative or quickly label anything gadget-related as an innovation.

Valuing constant invention has additional importance today, in an era of waning resources and environmental threats. In an interview with NBC News's Tom Brokaw following the 2008 Republican National Convention, Thomas L. Friedman responded to the issue of offshore drilling (a major topic in convention speeches,

which resulted in crowds chanting "drill, drill, drill"), calling instead for invention. He said: "America isn't sitting there saying 'invent, invent, invent . . . .' I'm actually not against drilling. What I'm against is making that the center of our focus, because we are on the eve of a new revolution, the energy technology revolution. It would be, Tom, as if on the eve of the IT revolution, the revolution of PCs and the Internet, someone was up there standing and demanding, 'IBM Selectric typewriters, IBM Selectric typewriters.' That's what 'drill, drill, drill' is the equivalent of today."[37]

Ingenuity, as opposed to innovation, is more personal, rooted in an individual's clever solutions to problems at hand. This relates directly to the well-known saying "necessity is the mother of invention," as ingenuity and invention often spring from the most dire situations. TV hero MacGyver, for example, was a pioneer of ingenuity, his gum-and-spit-bomb sensibilities inspiring many a DIY-er to make do with what she's got. While working in Uganda, a friend of mine took a photograph of a boy with a cast on each leg. The curvature of the casts made it nearly impossible for him to walk naturally, so his mother had fashioned convex shoe soles out of discarded tire treads and fastened them with rope. The solution was simple and ingenious, bringing immediate functionality to his situation. Many retail shoe companies have also used recycled tires as sole material, including Simple's line of Green Toe shoes, which I'm sure have been de-

A Ugandan boy with tire-tread shoes

scribed as innovative, not ingenious. Ingenuity and innovation are inherently tied to each other, but they differ in scale and scope. The means to bridge the two, however, and the tactic that will inform more empowering design solutions, is to innovate for ingenuity. As in The Designer's Handshake, the focus is collective efforts for and by individual action. We must collectively prioritize constant innovation, seeking out systemic solutions, but only as a means to empower individuals to use such design solutions to solve and serve their ongoing needs through ingenuity.

3.07 Need Before Consumption
Where there is a need, there is a market, and where there is a market, there are consumers. However, just as a square is a rectangle but a rectangle is not a square, just because something sells does not mean it is addressing a human need. In our own design practice, we must begin with the human need and ask questions like, "What is the problem and how can I best approach it?" and "What are the most basic needs that design can serve?"

When Kevin Murphy first conceptualized the Tack-Tiles Braille System, a block-based tool set for visually impaired learning, he was trying to serve the educational needs of his son, who is blind (see p. 180). Unable to find any adaptive tools for literacy, Murphy developed what would ultimately become a marketable product that facilitates learning for the blind in almost every academic subject and grade level. But he began by asking,

"What does my son need?" not, "What will sell?" That idea, of designing for needs first, should serve as a viable business and design model for maximizing social impact and long-term usability.

3.08 Consumption for Humanity
While much of this new model for need-based, human-centered design runs counter to the habits of consumerism, we can probably all agree that consumers and consumer culture are not going anywhere. And though the systems at work and the habits that feed them must change so that they value more long-lasting, adaptive, and necessary objects, we can in the meantime use consumption to our benefit, adapting commercially available products to suit our more basic needs. (You will notice that many of the products included in this book are consumer products.)

Apple's 3G iPhone, released in 2008, proved that technological functionality could be adapted to serve more humanitarian needs. The phone allows users to download applications, "apps," available for free or at a nominal cost through the iTunes store. The apps range from stock monitors and weather reports to games and educational tools (see p. 154). The educational applications are designed by outside companies and vendors, their subject matter ranging from astronomy and basic math to language lessons. With the development of the phone and these products, educational and academic learning experiences became seam-

lessly integrated into a consumer electronic offering.

Leapfrog, a longtime market leader in children's educational toys, partnered with the US Department of Health and Human Services to create an educational health book for Afghan women and children that uses the toy company's talking-book technology. Nintendo's Wii Fit makes home fitness fun, providing an activity interface through which individuals can improve and track personal health. Sony's "Buzz!" is a multiple-player quiz-based video game with trivia subjects ranging from the academic to pop-culture. "Buzz!" has been adapted for in-classroom use to facilitate interactive learning for children and provide an easy way for teachers to gauge students' comprehension. Myriad examples of such adaptation also exist in the developing world; for example, the use of cell phone technology to transmit medical records or negotiate agricultural trade prices across countries. So, while it is easy to dismiss consumerism as a force opposed to humanitarian design, it is actually a tool we can use to implement human-centered design solutions into a mainstream market while we work to make systematic changes in social practices and group mindsets.

3.09 Learning from Appropriate Technologies Engineering
Appropriate technologies is a field of engineering that designs, builds, and implements basic technological systems that are suitable for a particular location and the skills, materials, and

needs of a demographic. The discipline is based on three principles that designers should study and adapt: building as a generative process, the optimization of local resources, and using craft production as economic empowerment.

Building is widely recognized as an important cognitive process. Educational theories attest to the value of "constructionism" and "manipulatives" as the most effective ways for children to learn mathematical concepts because they form both mental and physical models, linking the tangible and the conceptual. Stanford University's Institute of Design (d.school) combines design education with entrepreneurship and business academics, offering studios including "Design for Extreme Affordability," in which students are encouraged to build their solutions at full scale, not just as a means to represent ideas, but in order to think, develop, and iteratively prototype.

The art of building as a generative design process, rather than simply one of model making, is not often seen, but it is inherent in appropriate technology engineering. Today, in a time of constant technological innovations, prototyping, modeling, and even preliminary sketching can conveniently be done in a variety of software programs. But working with your hands, physically understanding both the material and the way in which a user interacts with it, is indispensable to the design process. How can we ever understand the ways in which our clients and users will engage with the product if we as designers are not fully engaged in its realization?

Appropriate technologies are not only realized through building, but are also designed for, and with, a specific demographic of users. The Portable Light Project, which provides access to renewable energy by teaching craftspeople to stitch solar panels to traditional textile products, demonstrates the integration of innovation and local materials and skill sets beautifully. The idea behind it is an environmentally sensitive option, forcing designers to look to their surroundings, make use of waste products, and support local enterprises. It also creates a more direct relationship between designer and user that results in more personal solutions. We as designers can learn from this model, refocusing our efforts away from mass production toward more targeted, service-based, and locally inspired solutions that can be scaled and applied in other contexts. (Though the Portable Light Project began as a collaboration with Huichol women in the Sierra Madre region of Mexico, similar enterprises have since been implemented in Nicaragua, South Africa, and elsewhere.)

Appropriate technology engineering makes the case for craft as a viable business model for empowering communities, rather than merely a cultural expression. The Portable Light Project relies on traditional textile skills and integrates a training program to teach the technological integration of the solar panels, bringing added value to local skills. The program also trains weavers and creates jobs to support the production and distribution of the lights. This is the moment in which appropriate technologies and design become solutions, not just products. By capitalizing on existing skill sets and building training and support into design and enterprises, we give users not just a product (a solar-powered, portable light in a locally made textile), but also a solution (the ability to learn, read, or work in the evening, and even earn income from the production process).

3.10 User Engagement and Ownership

Given our throwaway culture—which encourages intense interest in, and then prompt disposal of, the latest products on the market—it's no wonder that people all too often feel no emotional connection to the object world. Particular to humanitarian design is a greater need for "co-created" design solutions that bring the user into the equation, creating a system by which the object is worthless without human interaction. Such products and systems are effective in two ways: Their creation forces the designer to put the user's engagement at the center of the design process, and in their use, the design makes the user a co-designer, increasing his ownership of and attachment to the product. This creates solutions that are longer lasting and more meaningful and that make the user experience an inte-

The Portable Light Project combines traditional craft and solar power to make nighttime education possible in off-the-grid locations

gral piece of the puzzle. Co-creation between designer and user results in more enabling and personal objects, as well as a more engaged and human-centered design process. From the first moment of design, user engagement requires that the end user be co-creator. The first rule of humanitarian design is to design with, not for, your client or community. If you're designing a new math toy for an educational think tank, bring young students to the table. If you're designing a low-cost water filter for a consumer water brand, talk to the rural communities who need it most. Most important, treat these clients, those the design is serving, with respect, compassion, and as the most important source of information and wisdom to inform the design solution. They are the project's resident experts.

At the point of use, a product also must require an engagement with its user. The Antivirus is an example of such a "half-product" whose function is dependent on a human action (see p. 90). The simple rubber cap must be attached properly to a standard aluminum soda can in order to facilitate the safe and sterile disposal of needle tips after a vaccine is administered. It's an important product that has implications to save lives, but without the human interaction, it is merely a rubber cap.

This engagement can also be financial, as a personal investment in the purchase of a product inherently makes the product more valuable to its owner. This is particularly relevant in the developing world, where many products, such as the Hippo Water Roller or the LifeStraw Family, are donated rather than purchased by the end user (see pp. 66, 72). User testing and research surveys demonstrate that sometimes these tools are not maintained because users view them as gifts rather than investments. The power of investing personal equity and ownership is a form of engagement that should be integrated into product distribution whenever possible, particularly in social enterprises and developing markets.

3.11 Design for the 100 Percent
I have a personal opposition to the term "design for the other 90 percent." Yes, you can quantitatively differentiate, in economic terms, the divide between the wealthy 10 percent (whom designers usually serve) and the underserved 90 percent, but there are problems with this approach. In its construction, the argument to design for the underserved is then inherently defined by difference. Also, the 90 percent has too often become synonymous with only impoverished residents of the developing world, when, in fact, the underserved is a much broader and more urgent category of people.

Because this entire argument is rooted in an "us-versus-them" mentality, it uses difference as a point of departure for the design process. In reality, what we need more than ever is inspiration through unity, a realization that our clients and users are co-creators, and that we as designers are also clients and users. This in no way implies that there is a universal design answer or that design cannot be personal and contextual. But design inspired by difference does not carry the same potential for impact as design inspired by commonality. We must look to opportunities to bridge markets and create unexpected partnerships that will result in shared investments, capital, and benefits.

The buy-one-give-one model employed by the aptly named BoGo Light from SunNight Solar is an example of a design approach that is supported by a bridging business model (see p. 122). The solar flashlight can be purchased online for personal use and the same flashlight will be distributed through a nonprofit partner to those in need of dependable light, including families living off the grid, the US Army, or schoolchildren in the developing world who can't study after dark.

However, while many of the other 90 percent are in the developing world, a good number of those people are also in our own backyards: the homeless, foster children, the handicapped, the elderly, inner-city public school students, and more. Design thinking should support the growth and economic empowerment of the "bottom of the pyramid" in the developing world while also tending to the needs of our own communities. Before traveling half way around the world, look for local design opportunities: Who is not being served in your own city? Could a design invest-

ment in your community help support a more productive and cohesive economy and culture?

The Los Angeles chapter of Project H, for instance, began an initiative called Abject Object, a collaboration with homeless shelter residents to design, produce, and sell retail textile objects. Though its aims and model have direct parallels with craft guild enterprises in Central America and microfinance-funded businesses in rural Africa, Abject Object is based in downtown Los Angeles, giving local people in need the skills, capital, and structure to help themselves.

3.12 A Brave New (Business) World
A design revolution will require new economic models within the design industry and support and investment from the business world. As social entrepreneurship models begin to prove that social value is economic value, designers have natural partners in the distribution and economic sustainability of life-improving design innovations. We must employ optimism and bravery in our business strategies, and apply design thinking, ingenuity, engineering, and business acumen in one fell swoop.

For many, design's role as a provider of wealth is paramount, but design as capital means providing a tool for someone to help herself out of poverty, start a business, produce enough to invest new equity, or otherwise turn a little into a lot. Luckily, social entrepreneurs support these same efforts in the distribution and production of tools (for agriculture,

Residents of the Downtown Women's Center weave products for sale through Abject Object

commerce, and health) that have quantifiable financial benefits for users. We must design not for wealth but for economic empowerment.

At the same time, we must continue to profit and pay our own bills. By bringing investors and social entrepreneurs to the design discussion at the outset, we can increase front-end capital, and by designing solutions that are income generators rather than donations for end users, we can build in repayment and microlending programs to minimize the distribution costs. Within our own practices, we can prove the value of design expertise and continue to be paid for our services by measuring and communicating the quantitative and qualitative benefits to potential clients. We must also look to local resources and skills and secondhand materials in our production cycles to cost-effectively and context-sensitively produce design solutions. And outside of the design bubble, we can work directly for nondesign entities to bring design thinking to the nonprofit arena and other social sectors.

We must also ensure that our designs are developed with viable distribution plans. Whether we mass produce, use the existing structure of a craft guild, or design a system for distributed manufacturing in which we deliver the tools for production of our concepts rather than the products themselves, the business model for distribution must be in place at the moment of design, not as an afterthought.

Finally, in order to solidify a financially supported structure for design for social impact, the design industry needs a public arm, and one not based on volunteering. While lawyers support legal aid and medical professionals support public health as integral to their industries, we, too, need an industry-supported sector to both broadcast our social values and to bring economic value to our humanitarian agendas. At the very least, a minimum commitment from each and every designer should be mandatory and built into the industry's framework. Papanek called for this nearly four decades ago, writing, "I think even the most successful designer can afford to give one-tenth of his time. It is unimportant what the mechanics of the situation are: four hours out of every 40, one working day out of every 10, or ideally, every 10th year to be spent as a sort of sabbatical, designing for many instead of designing for money."[38]

While Papanek's call-to-action still rings true, his last sentence will hopefully no longer be applicable in the coming years: Designing for many and designing for money need not be mutually exclusive. With new models for social entrepreneurship that are complementary to design ingenuity and that bring viable business and distribution partners, we can make design for social impact a profitable and sustainable enterprise for our users and ourselves.

3.13 Redefining the Design Client
Take a look at any design firm's website and you'll notice that the clients listed are primarily companies. Michael Graves's recent work for Drive Medical includes mobility and bath safety products (see p. 198). Graves, star architect and famed designer of products for retailers such as Target, was paralyzed from the midchest down several years ago. Because of his condition and mobility challenges, this new work poses solutions to help the elderly and disabled live and move more safely. The products, which range from bath seats to collapsible walking sticks, were designed for Drive Medical, the client, but the real clients are those who—like Graves— benefit from the products and whose mobility may be improved through their use.

While on paper we may continue to define the client as the person or company paying us, we must consider the client as the person or group we are serving and involve those people. In doing so, we will be able to refocus our efforts on the user experience and basic human needs, rather than catering solely to the brand, bank account, and priorities of the corporate client.

3.14 Design Outside of Design
After I started Project H and began lecturing about design as a tool for social change, young designers and design students would frequently ask me, "Who should I work for? Where can I get a job, design for the greater good, and still make money?" I would thoughtfully rack my brain and produce a list of five to eight firms, companies, or groups I truly believed to be doing good, socially relevant

design work, and recommend to the young designer that he check out the websites.

But after a while, I began wondering if this was the best advice. The design world is actually a very contained and self-supporting entity. At a conference late last year, when asked, "Who should I work for? What should I do?" I responded, in a sort of uncensored moment, "Don't work for a design firm." All this recent talk of design thinking, and yet most of the conversation was occurring within and for the design world itself. I went on, saying, "You want to use your design skills for good? Forget about designing stuff, and go work for a nonprofit, the government, or Amtrak." (I had just taken an abhorrent 42-hour train ride from San Francisco to Cleveland.)

If we as designers are as committed as we say we are to applying design thinking in places that truly need it, then let's do just that. Let's solve problems where they need solving— not in the confined loft office spaces we traditionally inhabit, but out in the world, in organizations, communities, and institutions that can benefit from design-based ideas. Let's rewrite our own job descriptions so that they may be applicable outside the design bubble, in places where design thinking is a scarce resource, and where creative problem solving has the greatest potential for impact.

At the same time, if we want to "take to the streets," we've got to know the streets and clearly define the limits of our own expertise and understanding. It is nothing short of arrogant for us to sit in our offices in London, New York, or San Francisco and assume we can design solutions to problems in rural Africa without taking the time to go there and understand the context. Fieldwork has become an afterthought, not a starting point. Whether we can ever really walk in someone else's shoes is debatable, but there is no question that, as designers, we have a duty to understand the people and environment for which we are designing as fully as possible before beginning to explore potential solutions.

3.15 Activism Through Academics

A design revolution must come from all sides and must start with education. The newest generation of citizen designers should have access to resources, including mentors, during their educations that will inform their values and priorities as they enter the workforce. More than ever, student designers are one of the few groups overwhelmingly filled with optimism and belief in the potential for design to ameliorate social ills and make life better.

And while universities are traditionally hotbeds of political and individual activism, that sense of purpose, drive, and confidence in change too often gets checked at the door of design studios. While studio programs may have a social slant, say, in the design of user-friendly tableware for the kitchen of 2020, they often lack a connection to a real world client or organization to bring the design to reality. Many designers will tell you

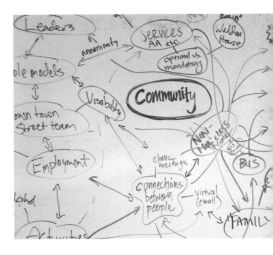

A brainstorming board from Stanford's d.school

MIT's D-Lab makes
charcoal from
sugarcane in Haiti

that not one of their student projects ever left the confines of their portfolio books of renderings, leaving some amazing ideas without real impact and implementation.

It seems to me, though, that design schools are *the* place to turn ideas into actionable realities because they combine student activism with an environment in which new concepts can be produced, critiqued, and developed. Archeworks, the self-proclaimed "alternative design school" in Chicago, was founded on this belief. Its program's design projects are carried out through partnerships with local nonprofits and other groups, providing a real client and a more viable stream of feedback by which to bring design solutions to particular users. Projects executed have included a redesigned pointing device for those with cerebral palsy and a kitchen concept for the disabled.

Stanford's d.school combines social entrepreneurship, product design, engineering, and business education in a studio program rooted in design thinking. Parsons the New School for Design in New York focused its 2003–8 thesis projects on design for good in an exhibition entitled *A Good Life,* in which each student partnered with a nonprofit to design a product or service for the organization's user group. Student projects included Christian John's Tessera, an educational puzzle for Iraqi refugee children, and Liza Forester's Let's Kick It program for DIY soccer balls (see pp. 270, 244). Perhaps the best example of design-as-action academics is MIT's D-Lab, an engineering-based course offering that creates simple and appropriate technologies for the developing world under the leadership of engineer and maverick Amy Smith. The lab's projects have included the previously mentioned sugarcane charcoal in Haiti and a low-cost lab test that uses a refashioned baby bottle and inexpensive filter paper to see if water is potable (see p. 74). Each of these academic initiatives is based on a social imperative and hands-on learning, and carried out through partnerships and strategic plans for implementation.

In looking to new models for design academics, we need the support of the academic institutions themselves. Colleges and universities need to take the initiative to put in place programs that are not simply socially oriented, but executable based on school, student, and public resources. And we need students to use their optimism and perseverance to not settle for the usual sketch-and-critique design academics. Students must demand access to avenues for research, implementation, feedback, and interdisciplinary collaboration.

3.16 Awareness and Visibility by Design

Designing tools that enable change starts with awareness, education, and measurement. What good is a tool if the user does not know how to use it or measure its success? The objects and systems we design must deliver solutions to problems and do so in a manner that is meaningful, adaptive,

and quietly didactic. Our approach must highlight and measure the problem, then propose a solution. By being formed through awareness, the solution carries more value and brings information, education, and understanding that subconsciously or consciously may inform an individual's use and adaptation of the solution.

Beginning in 2005, the British government began taking steps toward the widespread implementation of in-home Smart Meters, tools that measure and display energy consumption inside, rather than outside, the home. Research had shown that simply making the information readily available to users would result (and in test cases had resulted) in up to 10 percent reductions in energy consumption, without any other efforts.[39] The awareness alone was a habit-changer. Alex Steffen, founder of Worldchanging, calls this design for awareness "feedback-triggered change," by which the user reorients her actions toward efficiency and personal responsibility based on the availability and understanding of information (particularly as it pertains to her own footprint). More important, by making users aware, the smart choice becomes more obvious, even more convenient. "Making intelligent action the *easiest* choice is a powerful design strategy," asserts Steffen.[40] If more people are aware of their impacts through the design process, they are more likely to make informed decisions that will result in their own self-sufficiency and empowerment.

3.17 Beautiful Solutions to Ugly Problems

There's no denying that beauty is power. Like anything else, though, it's how you apply and prioritize beauty that matters. Many argue, and this is particularly true in design, that if something is beautiful, it is inherently valuable, but I assert that beauty is merely an enhancement to that which already has value.

On a recent trip to New York, I took a tour of KIPP Infinity, a charter school in Harlem where a friend of mine teaches seventh-grade English. The school's walls are painted in vibrant colors (by the teachers and students) and adorned with artwork, posters, and inspiring quotes. Classrooms proudly display the flags of the colleges and universities from which the teachers graduated, while sofas and warm lighting create inviting nooks in which children can read or just hang out. It is truly a beautiful place, and it is no coincidence that the fifth- to eighth-grade students looked happy and inspired. As my friend described how the school works, the rigorous curriculum, and the caliber of the teaching talent, I realized it was not just the colored walls that made the school successful. The committed teachers and students, backed by a pioneering nonprofit charter school system, made it run. The engaging physical environment was both a product of those systems and a catalyst to maintain and inspire further educational success.

Danish company Aresa Biodetec-

tion has brought an enhanced design solution to some of the world's most violent areas through a genetically modified species of plant that changes color when its roots grow in the vicinity of explosive landmines. The roots turn red when they are in contact with nitrogen dioxide, which is produced by the explosive devices as the chemicals decay. In this case, the beauty—the changing of the plant's color—is merely a tool to visually represent a scientific solution. In other words, beauty is an instrument to help implement a solution and make it more usable. Let us look to beauty as a means to catalyze already great ideas, but not prioritize beauty over function or human relevance.

3.18 Small Stories and the User as Paramount

A final thought: Yes, this book proclaims that design can change the world. And it's an asset to dream big and think good. "Perpetual optimism is a force multiplier," says former secretary of state Colin Powell.[41] But

while thinking big we must always remember that design is for people: your grandmother and your neighbor, a farmer, a squatter, a prisoner, and an average Joe. The singular user is paramount. Design succeeds when it begins with small stories and is later scaled to produce a larger impact that is at the same time global and personal. One of the founding members of design collective Droog, Renny Ramakers, wrote in a sort of mission statement and manifesto for the initiative, "Now it is the turn of small stories, rooted in everyday reality. Stories that tell of products capable of aging gracefully and allowing the user to bond with them, of the value of things that already exist, of personal ecology, of uncertainty, dreams, passion, and pleasure."[42]

Despite our own individual personal agendas of world-changing design, let us always begin with one: It is for and by our users that our designs are inspired, exist, fail, succeed, grow, and change. My hope with this book is to tell a few of those stories, to make

the case for user-centered, humanitarian design, perhaps to change your idea of what design is and could be, and to inspire you to act accordingly.

1. United Nations, *The Millennium Development Goals Report*, New York: 2005, http://unstats.un.org/unsd/mi/pdf/MDG%20Book.pdf.

2. Victor Papanek, *Design for the Real World: Human Ecology and Social Change*, 2nd ed. (Chicago: Academy Chicago Publishers, 1985), 86.

3. Allan Chochinov, "1000 Words: A Manifesto for Sustainability in Design," April 2007, http://www.core77.com/reactor/04.07_chochinov.asp.

4. Ibid., ix.

5. US Consumer Product Safety Commission, "Fisher-Price Recalls Licensed Character Toys Due to Lead Poisoning Hazard," August 2, 2007, http://www.cpsc.gov/cpscpub/prerel/prhtml07/07257.html.

6. *The Incredibles*, Brad Bird, dir. and perf. (voice of Edna Mode), Pixar Animation Studios, 2004.

7. Bryan Bell, "Expanding Design toward Greater Relevance," in Bryan Bell and Katie Wakeford, eds., *Expanding Architecture: Design as Activism* (New York: Metropolis Books, 2008), 15.

8. Jeff Karoub, "Critics Turning Green over Overused Words," *Sacramento Bee*, December 31, 2008.

9. EarthTalk, *E/The Environmental Magazine*, June 29, 2008, http://www.emagazine.com/view/?4277&src.

10. IDEO and The Rockefeller Foundation, *Design for Social Impact: How-to Guide*, https://client.ideo.com/socialimpact/docs/IDEO_RF_Guide.pdf.

11. Paul Polak, "Design for the Other Ninety Percent," in Cynthia E. Smith, ed., *Design for the Other 90%* (New York: Cooper-Hewitt, National Design Museum, Smithsonian Institution, 2007), 19.

12. Thomas L. Friedman, *The World Is Flat: A Brief History of the Twenty-first Century* (New York: Farrar, Straus, and Giroux, 2006).

13. Jamais Cascio, "Leapfrog 101," Worldchanging, December 15, 2004, http://www.worldchanging.com/archives/001743.html.

14. Steven Heller, introduction to Steven Heller and Véronique Vienne, eds., *Citizen Designer: Perspectives on Design Responsibility* (New York: Allworth Press, 2003), ix.

15. Ibid., xi.

16. Stanley Tigerman, interview with Cheryl Towler Weese, *inForm*, vol. 13, no. 2, 2001.

17. Tim Brown, "Strategy by Design," *Fast Company*, June 2005.

18. Ibid.

19. Tate Museum, "Damien Hirst: Pharmacy," http://www.tate.org.uk/pharmacy.

20. Thomas Fisher, "Public-Interest Architecture: A Needed and Inevitable Change," in Bell and Wakeford, eds., 12.

21. Kiva, "Facts & Statistics," http://www.kiva.org/about/help/stats.

22. Grameen Bank, "Grameen Bank At-A-Glance," http://grameen-info.org/index.php?option=com_content&task=view&id=26&Itemid=175.

23. KickStart, "KickStart," http://www.kickstart.org.

24. KickStart, "KickStart: What We Do: Our Impact," http://www.kickstart.org/what-we-do/impact.

25. Architecture for Humanity, ed., *Design Like You Give a Damn: Architectural Responses to Humanitarian Crises* (New York: Metropolis Books, 2006).

26. Cameron Sinclair, "I Hope It's a Long List . . .," in Architecture for Humanity, ed., 31.

27. Valerie Casey, Compostmodern Conference, San Francisco, January 19, 2008.

28. Valerie Casey, "The Designer's Dilemma," *design mind*, summer 2007.

29. Ibid.

30. David Roberts, "Green So Light It Barely Leaves an Impression," *Grist*, April 30, 2007, http://gristmill.grist.org/story/2007/4/30/144718/892.

31. Wal-Mart, "S*Mart Sustainability Newsletter," August 2007, http://walmartstores.com/download/2628.pdf.

32. Julie Gallagher, "Wal-Mart's Gaining Green Momentum," *Supermarket News*, January 29, 2008, http://subscribers.supermarketnews.com/Grocery_Center_Store_Brands/walmarts_gaining_green/index.html.

33. Scott Anderson, *The Man Who Tried to Save the World: The Dangerous Life and Mysterious Disappearance of an American Hero* (New York: Anchor, 2000).

34. Online Ethics Center at the National Academy of Engineering, "Fred Cuny (1944–1995)—Disaster Relief Innovator: Ethiopia (1985): Famine," http://www.onlineethics.org/cms/14196.aspx.

35. D-Lab at the Massachusetts Institute of Technology, "Fuel from the Fields: A Guide to Converting Agricultural Waste into Charcoal Briquettes," October 20, 2004, http://web.mit.edu/d-lab/portfolio/charcoal/Sugarcane%20Charcoal%20Manual%20Draft%20October%202004.doc.

36. Lauri Puchall, "Tomb with a View: Frederick Law Olmsted's Eternal Vision for Oakland's Mountain View Cemetery," *The Monthly*, July 2007.

37. Thomas L. Friedman, interview by Tom Brokaw, *Meet the Press*, NBC, September 7, 2008.

38. Papanek, 69.

39. Smart Meters, "Emissions Reduction Goals Won't Be Met without Smart Meters," http://www.smartmeters.com/news/Emissions-reduction-goals-won't-be-met-without-smart-meters-n339.html.

40. Alex Steffen, "Smart Meters," Worldchanging, May 19, 2006, http://www.worldchanging.com/archives/004451.html.

41. Colin Powell with Joseph L. Persico, *My American Journey* (New York: Random House, 1995).

42. Renny Ramakers, *Droog Design 2* (Rotterdam: 010 Publishers, 2002).

water

Air2Water Dolphin 2 / dragonfly M18

Air2Water's Dolphin 2/dragonfly M18 is a compact countertop device that provides membrane-filtered, UV-purified, and treated water by literally making it out of thin air. Using the company's patented Aquovate technology, the M18 converts ambient atmospheric water vapor into potable water by treating it with advanced purification techniques.

While most home water filters purify tap water, the M18 pulls moisture directly from the air. Air passes through a filter and then condenses into water, which is collected in a tank. This condensation process may also be bypassed simply by filling the collection tank with tap water. The water is then sent through the system's Hyflux filtration cartridges and optional UV lamp to remove waterborne contaminants including bacteria, parasites, and viruses. Water is now ready to be dispensed. To avoid stagnation and ensure freshness, the M18 also recirculates water to the collection tank.

designer:
Air2Water
geographical implementation/ market/availability:
Global, via dealers
status:
Consumer product
price:
$2,000 and up
website:
www.air2water.net

Air Wash

The AirWash waterless washing machine offers a water-wise standard for future home appliances, even though it is currently only a prototype concept. Inspired by nature's cleansing agents and the dirt-sucking technology of air filters, the AirWash uses negative ions and atmospheric air—rather than water and detergents—to clean clothes. Its form is meant to resemble a waterfall, which produces negative ions and natural cleansing power through its cascading water.

Designed for the 2005 Electrolux Design Lab Competition by two students in the industrial design program at the National University of Singapore, the prototype would channel air currents and negative ions to pull impurities, odor, and dirt from cloth fibers. While the technology has yet to be resolved, the concept took first prize in the competition, signifying a shift in design priorities to more resource-independent and environmentally responsible home appliances.

Established in 2003, the Electrolux Design Lab Competition for industrial design students encourages entrants to submit innovative, daring ideas that reimagine home appliances and address current limitations in the market.

designers:
Wendy Chua, Gabriel Tan
other partners/clients/producers:
Electrolux Design Lab Competition
status:
Concept
website:
www.electrolux.com/designlab

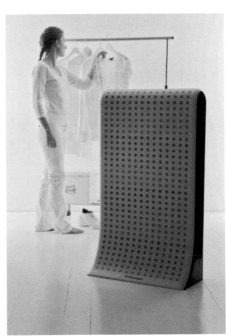

Aquacube Containerized Water Treatment Plants

With applications for peacekeeping, disaster, off-the-grid, horticultural, and municipal situations, Aquacube Containerized Water Treatment Plants take clean water where it is most needed. Systems developed by DPM Water Technologies for filtration, reverse osmosis, desalination, and disinfection are all integrated into an easy-to-operate, self-contained system that works with a variety of water sources and in multiple terrains and climates. Bag, cartridge, mixed-media, and sand filters remove particles from water, while activated carbon eliminates dissolved chemicals. Chlorination, electrochlorination, and

UV lamps destroy microbiological contaminants, including bacteria and viruses, and reverse osmosis systems dissolve salt, leaving brackish water pure and clean.

The combination of these technologies results in a clean water supply suitable for irrigation, industrial applications, or drinking. Standard shipping containers act as a widely available and universal building block within which the water treatment plants are assembled. The standardized format also enables the Aquacube to produce high volumes of treated water with minimal infrastructure needs.

designer:
  DPM Water Technologies, Ltd.
**geographical implementation/
market/availability:**
  Global, via website
status:
  Limited distribution
website:
  www.aquacube.org.uk

Aquaduct

designer:
    IDEO
other partners/clients/producers:
    Innovate or Die Pedal-Powered
    Machine Contest
**geographical implementation/
market/availability:**
    Global
status:
    Concept
website:
    www.ideo.com

page 54
Design Revolution
water
+ mobility

During a three-week design charrette, five engineers and designers from IDEO created Aquaduct, a bicycle intended to transport, filter, and store water in the developing world. The concept vehicle was an entrant in, and winner of, the Innovate or Die Pedal-Powered Machine Contest hosted by Goodby, Silverstein & Partners, Google, and Specialized Bicycles. In parts of the developing world where access to clean drinking water is scarce, the Aquaduct aims to provide filtered water by using the pedal power of a bicycle, a familiar source of transportation within those demographics.

Billions of people struggle with both water access (as it can take hours to walk to the source) and filtration, and the Aquaduct is a single-vehicle solution to those problems. The bicycle can be ridden, like any other, to the water source, where the large tank is filled. As the rider pedals, the motion activates a pump that moves water from the tank through a filter and into a smaller, clean-water holding tank.

The smaller tank can also be removed to function within the home as a water storage unit and dispenser.

The functioning prototype was designed and constructed for the contest, and IDEO intends to further develop the concept into a marketable, affordable, and technologically innovative product to distribute globally. The market version will address issues of cost viability as well as the suitability and maintainability of purification techniques. The Aquaduct's design offers a widely applicable strategy to help solve a problem that affects a significant portion of the global population.

AquaPak

The AquaPak bag is a portable and cost-effective solution to the problem of contaminated water in off-the-grid, rural, and developing areas. The product uses the sun's rays to eliminate bacteria, viruses, and parasitic pathogens, including cholera and salmonella, from fresh water. AquaPak is reliant only on sunlight, thereby making pasteurization technology a viable technique for the provision of potable water.

designer:
   Solar Solutions Laboratories
geographical implementation/ market/availability:
   Global, via website
status:
   Consumer product
price:
   $19.95
website:
   www.solarsolutions.info

Made from a low-cost polyethylene with UV inhibitors, the sealable bag has transparent bubble-pack sheeting on one side and an opaque black surface on the other. The black side aids in the heating of the water to a temperature of 152 °F (67 °C), which, if maintained for 15 minutes, will reduce the presence of all pathogens by 99.999 percent. To ensure that the water gets this hot, the bag comes with a built-in, glass tube indicator filled with colored wax that melts when heated to the required temperature. Depending on the availability of steady sunlight throughout the day, an AquaPak bag can produce up to 4 gallons (15 L) of safe drinking water, enough for a family of four for one day.

Brita Filters

Brita has long been a leader in providing in-home water filtration solutions that are affordable, healthy, and high quality. The company began in 1966 when German entrepreneur Heinz Hankammer set out to optimize tap water. His first filter, AquaDeMat, was used in garages throughout Europe to demineralize water for car batteries. The venture grew into the modern-day company, named after his daughter, and now includes a comprehensive product line of pitchers, faucet mounts, and refrigerator filters for a global consumer market.

Brita filters reduce lead, copper, mercury, and chlorine tastes and odors, without adding sodium. The filters, which can process 40 gallons (151 L) of water before requiring replacement, use activated carbon and an ion-exchange resin. The carbon is made from coconut shells through a special heating process that increases the surface area and pore size of the shells for maximum absorption of impurities, while the resin acts like a magnet to pull lead, copper, mercury, cadmium, and zinc particles out of tap water. Faucet-mount filtration systems also remove microbiological cysts including giardia and cryptosporidium. Brita Smart Pitchers allow users to monitor the effectiveness of filters and replace them as soon as they are no longer functional.

FilterForGood, Brita's campaign to reduce water-bottle waste, asks consumers to pledge their commitment to using in-home filters and reusable vessels, reducing usage of plastic water bottles and raising awareness of water health and conservation. FilterForGood partners include Country Time, Crystal Light, Kool-Aid, and Nalgene.

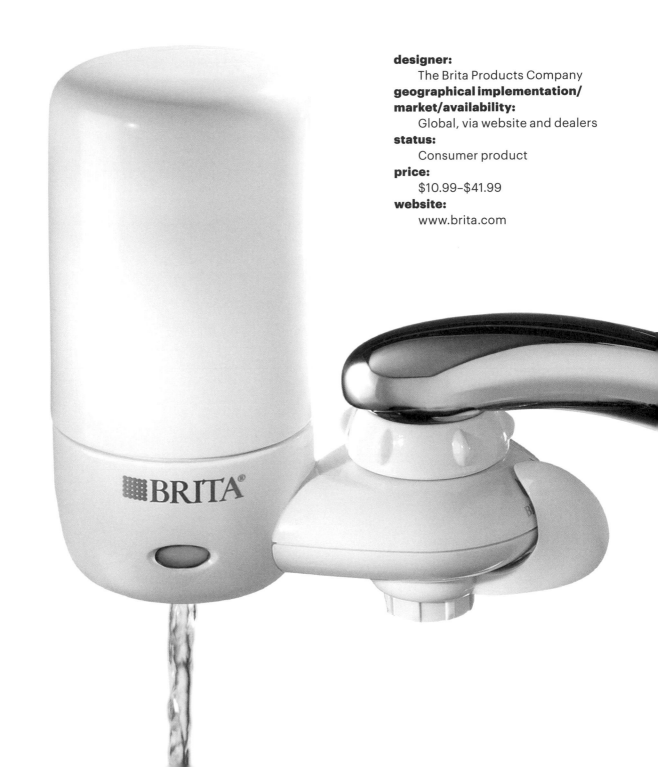

designer:
The Brita Products Company
**geographical implementation/
market/availability:**
Global, via website and dealers
status:
Consumer product
price:
$10.99–$41.99
website:
www.brita.com

Clay
Water
Filters

designer:
　Tony Flynn
other partners/clients/producers:
　The Australian National University
geographical implementation/
market/availability:
　Global
status:
　DIY
price:
　Cost of materials
website:
　www.anu.edu.au

A grassroots alternative to higher-tech filtration systems, Tony Flynn's three-ingredient filters take advantage of the inherent properties of locally available materials to provide clean drinking water in the simplest of manners. Flynn, a materials scientist and ceramics lecturer from The Australian National University, combined terra-cotta, coffee grounds (or other organic material), and cow dung to create personal-use water filters that remove common pathogens including E. coli. The filters provide a free, do-it-yourself alternative to the commercial options, which often use the same ceramic filtration process but are financially inaccessible to developing communities.

The filters can be made by anyone with access to crushed terra-cotta, organic material, and sufficient water to create a thick mixture that can be formed into a self-supported pot. The shaped pots are sun dried until hard, then fired on a bed of dry cow dung and leaves for 45 minutes. During the firing process, the organic material burns out, leaving small pores in the pot through which water will pass but pathogens will not. Dry cow dung, a highly efficient and hot-burning fuel, reaches a temperature of 1,742 °F (950 °C) in less than 30 minutes during the open-firing process, burning hotter and faster than traditional ceramic kilns.

While most ceramicists argue that clay's porosity is a hindrance to filtration, Flynn's filters take advantage of this material property, along with the wide availability of organic material and agricultural by-products in the demographics for which DIY filters are most urgently needed. The filters safely remove 96.4 to 99.8 percent of all E. coli bacteria and can filter .25 gallon (1 L) of water in two hours. Several filters may be used in sequence for particularly contaminated or dirty water. Perhaps the system's only drawback is the difficulty of perfecting the mixture, wall thickness, and shape of the pots, all of which can require some practice. Those with previous ceramics or craft experience will be better equipped to produce higher-quality filters.

Here is how to do it yourself:

1. Make the clay mixture.
Crush reddish brown terra-cotta into a powder. Mix one handful with one handful of dry, organic material (preferably coffee grounds, rice hulls, or tea leaves). Add water until the mixture is firm enough to be handled and shaped.

2. Shape into pots and make the fire.
Shape the clay into a cylindrical pot with an opening of about 4 inches (10 cm) in diameter. The wall of the pot should be as thick as a finger. Let the pots sun dry. Create piles of dry cow manure and place the dried pots on top of them. Surround the pots with straw or leaves and add two to three more layers of manure. The pots should be completely covered. Light the straw or leaves.

3. Add more manure to the fire.
The fire will reach approximately 1,292 °F (700 °C) in 30 minutes, and will reach 1,652 to 1,742 °F (900 to 950 °C) after 50 to 60 minutes. Add more manure, covering any holes in the mound, to keep the fire hot. The fire should burn a bright orange to yellow color. The filters should fire at that color for at least 30 minutes.

4. Bake the filters and remove them from the fire.
After 45 to 50 minutes the organic material will burn away and the pots can be removed. They will be red hot, so do not touch them. More pots can be put on the fire at this time and covered with additional manure.

5. Filter water.
Allow the filter to cool. Rinse out any charcoal or dirt and fill with water. After the first round of water is discarded, filters are safe and ready to use. The filters can be held or set atop bottles or glasses to catch the clean water during the filtration process.

Eco-Machines

designer:
Todd Ecological, Inc.
other partners/clients/producers:
Ocean Arks International
geographical implementation/
market/availability:
Global, on project basis
status:
Limited distribution
website:
www.toddecological.com

Dr. John Todd, founder and senior partner of Todd Ecological and self-proclaimed "biological explorer and ecological designer," believes that by partnering with nature, harnessing its power, and understanding its processes, we can reduce our negative environmental footprint by 90 percent. Eco-Machines are miniature ecosystems that use flora, fauna, and bacteria to naturally cleanse water, treat sewage, and turn wastewater and material into fuel and food. Todd sees these natural cleansing methods as a viable and obvious alternative to the current predominant methods of treating water, which require over-engineering, toxic chemicals, and excessive energy usage.

Each Eco-Machine is tailored to its surroundings, client, and required application. Installations have included an aquaculture system that turns fish waste into nutrients to grow vegetables, a 1,968-foot (600-m) system to depollute an urban canal in China, and a laboratory for hands-on education at Berea College in Kentucky.

In the Eco-Machine's waste treatment system, a series of tanks works in sequence using different combinations of organisms. As wastewater passes from one tank to the next, it gets progressively cleaner, so by the end it can be used for irrigation. The organisms and plant species in each Eco-Machine are selected individually to increase the efficiency and ecological performance of the specific system and its surroundings. The goal is to mimic the environment as closely as possible, creating a "microcosm of the macrocosm" by including many of nature's most important fundamental elements, such as microbial and photosynthetic communities, linked ecosystems, mineral complexity, and nutrient and micronutrient reservoirs that support biological diversity.

Eco-Machines rely on the strategic application of nature's most beneficial and generative purification processes for water and pollution remediation. To date the systems have been designed to generate fuel, grow food, repair damaged environments, regulate climates, and treat toxic waste. Todd views the approach as socially and environmentally responsible, not to mention good sense. "Evolution is two billion years of research and development," he states. "We do not manage nature. We, at best, partner with it."

Envirolet
FlushSmart VF

While the idea of a waterless, composting toilet may not be immediately appealing, Envirolet's Vacuum FlushSmart systems combine the environmental benefits of waste composting with a low-flush, traditional toilet. The result is an efficient and eco-friendly fusion of sanitation techniques that is a comfortable step toward solid-waste composting for the average consumer. The FlushSmart system moves waste via suction into a composting vessel that can be placed above, below, or level with the toilet, making installation easy in any home. The three-component system utilizes a VacuFlush Toilet and a Vacuum Generator Unit from Dometic Group, along with an Envirolet composting unit. The entire product uses less than .13 gallon (.5 L) of water per flush and is available with pedal- or electronic-flush functions.

When the toilet is flushed, the Vacuum Generator Unit pulls the waste from the toilet into the composting unit. During this process waste is aerated and pulverized. Out-side air enters, is heated, and forced into the tray area of the composting system. Here, the patented Automatic Six-Way Aeration process ventilates the waste from six sides, allowing for maximum air flow for rapid evaporation and composting.

The evaporation of liquids occurs quickly, leaving behind the solid waste to compost. This remaining solid material sits in a warm, confined, and well-aerated environment. Additives including peat moss, compost accelerator, and rich soil may be used to speed up the natural microbial functions that occur throughout the composting process. The resulting compost may be utilized like any other.

Envirolet Composting Toilets have been sold worldwide since 1977 and are manufactured and marketed by Sancor Industries. Their product range includes composting, water-less, and vacuum-flush toilets for virtually every application, from large home to cabin, cabana, and workspace.

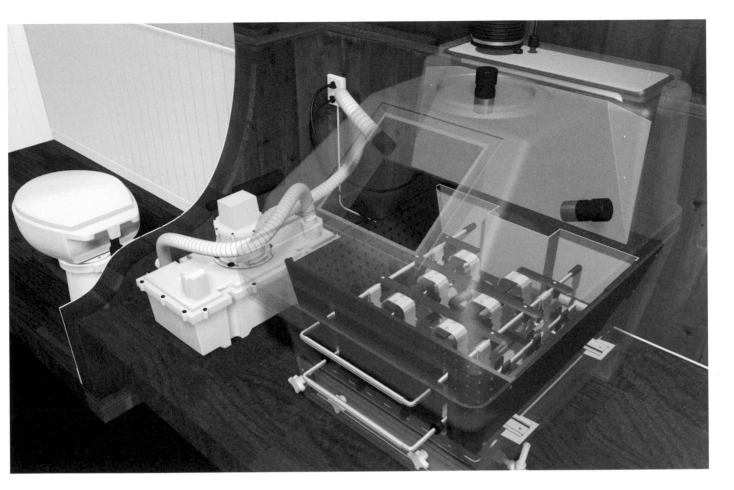

designer:
Envirolet
**geographical implementation/
market/availability:**
Global, via website and catalogue
status:
Consumer product
price:
$3,199–$3,699
website:
www.envirolet.com

Hippo Water Roller

designers:
Johan Jonker, Pettie Petzer
other partners/clients/producers:
Imvubu Products
geographical implementation/
market/availability:
Global, by donation
status:
Limited distribution
price:
$90
website:
www.hipporoller.org

In the developing world, millions of people struggle to survive without reliable access to water. Women and children are traditionally responsible for fetching water, sometimes up to three times daily and from sources up to 5 miles (8 km) away. Water transport devices range from wheelbarrows to jerricans, discarded bottles, and gas cans. Carrying water on one's head, a common practice in these areas, can result in serious cranial and spinal injuries that chronically afflict the young and elderly.

The Hippo Water Roller, designed in 1991 by South Africans Johan Jonker and Pettie Petzer, provides a safe and efficient alternative. The rotationally molded, UV-sterilized, polyethylene barrel holds approximately 24 gallons (90 L) of water, compared to the 2.5- to 5-gallon (10- to 20-L) capacity of traditional methods. One trip with the Hippo Roller transports enough water for a family of five to seven for up to one week.

The Hippo Roller's detachable steel handle allows for easy assembly and disassembly. Although the barrel has an effective weight of 40 pounds (18 kg) when full, the handle also makes it easy enough for a child to use on flat terrain. Sturdy construction gives the barrels life spans of up to seven years.

Beyond the Hippo Roller's immediate function and efficiency, its implementation has resulted in quantifiable, tangible social impact in parts of South Africa. In communities that use the Hippo Roller, men have begun to view fetching water as a more masculine, worthwhile chore. Correspondingly, education and literacy rates for women and children in the communities have improved, and female-run businesses have become much more commonplace.

Since 1991 more than 27,000 Hippo Rollers have been distributed throughout Africa, with the majority in use in South Africa. The product's design has been improved during various re-prototyping phases, with the most recent version conceptualized by pro bono designers

from Project H Design, a global product design nonprofit, and the
San Francisco chapter of Engineers
Without Borders. The new Hippo
Roller will maximize shipping efficiencies, lower price points as a means
to increase distribution and ownership possibilities, and improve the
product's water-tight performance.

LIFESAVER Bottle

While there are many water filters for camping, mountaineering, and developing markets, the LIFESAVER Bottle combines a filter and drinking vessel in an army-grade, portable, safe-water device. The all-in-one ultrafiltration bottle removes bacteria, viruses, parasites, fungi, and all other microbiological, waterborne pathogens, without chemicals such as iodine or chlorine.

The 1.6-pint (750-ml) bottle works quickly and safely: The user unscrews the bottom of the bottle, fills and closes it, activates the filter using the internal pump mechanism, and drinks from the chew-proof nozzle. Replaceable cartridges are available in 1,050- to 1,585-gallon (4,000- to 6,000-L) capacities, while universal instructions demonstrate proper usage, maintenance, and cleaning through graphics rather than words. Using LIFESAVER's unique FAILSAFE technology, the bottle's cartridge automatically ceases to work upon the filter's expiry, providing self-regulation that prevents the consumption of contaminated water.

This double-use technology in a single product has applications for off-the-grid and disaster situations, as well as in developing and rural markets where clean water is not easily accessible.

designer:
LIFESAVER Systems
geographical implementation/ market/availability:
Global, via website
status:
Consumer product
price:
$229
website:
www.lifesaversystems.com

LifeStraw Personal and Family

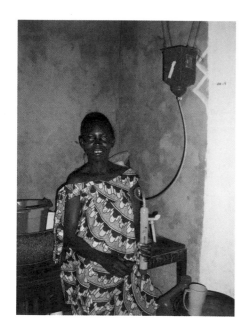

Following the success of, and media attention given to, the LifeStraw Personal—a portable water purifier that works as a straw to transform potentially contaminated water into potable water by the time the liquid hits a user's lips—Danish company Vestergaard Frandsen released the LifeStraw Family system. Half of the world's poor suffer from waterborne diseases. To help address this staggering problem, the LifeStraw Family provides an instant, microbiological, point-of-use, in-home filtration system that complements the personal filter, producing up to 4,750 gallons (18,000 L) of clean water in its lifetime. The system was created in alignment with the United Nations' Millennium Development Goals for global health and poverty eradication to help halve the number of people without sustainable access to safe drinking water by the year 2015.

LifeStraw Family has a high-flow rate and removes 99.9999 percent of all bacteria, 99.99 percent of all viruses, and 99.9 percent of all para-

sites. Unlike similar systems, LifeStraw Family works on highly turbid water, making it applicable in both rural and dense urban contexts. It requires no power, batteries, or spare parts and is easy to clean and maintain within the home.

The system consists of a bucket, which should be hung high, and a tube that connects to the strawlike filtering tool. The device uses an integrated filtration system, pump, and tap to purify water efficiently. Dirty water is poured into the bucket, and gravity forces it through the connecting tube into the purification cartridge. Within the cartridge, millions of pores, called capillary membranes, remove contaminants as water flows through them. Clean water is then ready to be dispensed from the attached tap. Collected dirt is released from the bottom of the cartridge by squeezing the device's bulb after use. When used properly, the device filters an average of 2.6 gallons (10 L) of water per hour. At $20 per unit, LifeStraw Family is low cost compared

designer:
Vestergaard Frandsen
**geographical implementation/
market/availability:**
Global, via website
status:
Limited distribution
price:
$20, minimum order 100 units
website:
www.vestergaard-frandsen.com

to other point-of-use products with similar life cycles.

In a pilot study in the Democratic Republic of the Congo, the product was given to 10 families who had significantly limited access to safe drinking water. After one month of daily usage, the units showed no signs of damage or malfunction and recorded flow rates of 0.25 gallon (1 L) in less than five minutes. Most important, users found them easy to use, clean, and maintain, and reported decreased incidents of diarrhea within their families. There are four billion cases of waterborne diarrhea annually worldwide, but LifeStraw Family's reliable in-home system works to address the problem by helping increase water safety and health among communities in need.

Low-Cost Water Testing

MIT's D-Lab is a class, curriculum, team, and think-tank of engineering students creating innovative and affordable solutions that address the problems of the world's most impoverished citizens. Their Low-Cost Water Test is one of many projects whose development and implementation was spearheaded by director Amy Smith and carried out through a collaboration between students and professionals. The test has been used in Haiti, Honduras, and Pakistan, providing an affordable alternative to other water-testing devices that can cost up to $1,000.

Many people in the developing world have access to water but no way to determine if it is safe to drink. Most water-testing devices used in labs employ replaceable filters and filter paper that show water's potability. D-Lab found that baby bottles can act as replacements for the least important component of that process—the vessel in which the water is tested—since the mouths of the bottles are the same dimension, within millimeters, as that of the circular filter papers. The bottle then becomes a reusable vessel, fitted with single-use components for repeated sterile use.

To begin the process, a disposable, sterile bottle insert is placed inside the baby bottle and is filled with the water to be tested. The filter paper is placed on top of the bottle's opening and held in place by the cap. The bottle is turned upside down, and using a syringe attached to the bottle, the water is sucked through the filter paper. The filter is then removed and placed in a petri dish to process in an incubator for 24 hours. The filter paper may then be read by technicians to detect any water contamination. This alternative system uses pre-existing products readily available in the developing world to deliver a reliable result.

designer:
D-Lab at the Massachusetts Institute of Technology (MIT)
geographical implementation/ market/availability:
Haiti, Honduras, Pakistan; on project basis
status:
Project implemented
price:
System approx. $10; water tests $0.02–$0.03 each
website:
web.mit.edu/d-lab

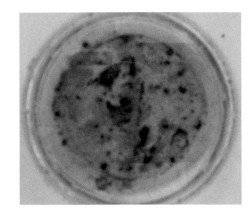

Rainwater Catchment Systems

**geographical implementation/
market/availability:**
Global
status:
DIY
price:
Cost of materials
websites:
Resources at
www.harvesth2o.com
www.rainwaterharvesting.tamu.edu
www.gardenwatersaver.com

Think of rain as a giant faucet—a free water supply ready to be gathered. As a means to both conserve municipal water supplies and access a sustainable source of fresh water, rainwater harvesting is a robust and viable option that works almost universally. Catchment systems can function in many geographical contexts and on scales ranging from single-family homes in the developing world to large industrial and architectural applications in the developed world. Particularly in cities—where concrete and other nonpermeable surfaces contribute to the runoff of uncaptured rain, which erodes soil and carries chemicals directly into oceans and lakes—a proper catchment system can provide households with a significant amount of water for landscaping and other nonpotable outdoor uses. Rainwater is free of salts and other harmful minerals, so it does not have to be treated for such purposes. (It can be filtered after collection for potability.) In this way rainwater can reduce the amount of new fresh water required in a home.

The relatively simple catchment system consists of a surface for collecting rainwater, a place to store or distribute the water, and a conduit to pipe the water from its collection point to its storage point. For some uses, such as irrigation, the system can be set up to bypass the storage component and directly distribute the water. Systems work in the same manner regardless of their geographical contexts. In the developing world, many households channel water from a corrugated roof into jerricans or buckets using conduits such as papyrus reeds, PVC tubing, chains, or even rope or fabric.

To build your own catchment system, follow these basic steps and access the listed websites for further information:

1. Collect and direct it.
Most modern homes have a built-in gutter or downspout system, which makes the integration of a rainwater catchment system fairly easy. The simplest way to channel rainwater into a storage tank is to cut or redirect a downspout or use a diverting device specifically designed for the purpose, such as the Garden Watersaver. If you are using a downspout, simply place the storage tank directly beneath it, leaving a little room between the opening and the tank.

2. Filter it.
The rainwater has just traveled through the gutter system, so it likely has collected bugs, leaves, or other debris. Before the rainwater is stored in its tank, a basic filtration system should be employed to remove such matter. This can range from a simple screen placed at the end of the downspout to a fine-mesh screen that covers the mouth of the storage container.

3. Store it.
Many types of storage vessels can be used, from empty wine barrels to sanitized oil drums and specifically designed plastic rain barrels. The aesthetics are less important than the size, which should be large enough to accommodate rainwater from a heavy downpour and to hold sufficient water for your landscaping purposes. If immediate distribution is necessary, the container should be elevated to avoid the need for a pump.

4. Distribute it.
To facilitate irrigation, some commercially available rainwater storage units may have a built-in valve at the bottom of the container, making collection and transport of smaller quantities of water easy. For garden applications, a small bucket can be filled and carried to where the water is needed. If the storage container is aboveground, there are a variety of gravity-fed, channel, or drip irrigation systems that can efficiently move rainwater throughout your landscape.

5. Maintain it.
Monitor the rainwater collection vessel closely, checking for insect or mosquito breeding and buildup of algae and other debris. Gutters should be cleaned regularly, and the structural integrity of any aboveground container systems should be ensured.

ROVAI Rope Pump

Communities in the developing world continually need simple technologies to bring groundwater to the surface for drinking or irrigation uses. The rope pump, first used by the Chinese thousands of years ago, is a common system that pumps water from a shallow well using basic materials and minimal labor.

In Cambodia, Ideas at Work collaborated with RDIC to develop the ROVAI rope pump, a system optimized for simple construction techniques and materials that works at well depths of up to 66 feet (20 m), producing approximately 10.5 gallons (40 L) of water per minute at a depth of 16 feet (5 m). The ROVAI pump (*rovai* is Khmer meaning "to turn something by hand") is made from a long loop of rope, stock steel that is readily available all over the world, standard PVC piping, and pistons that are formed through a small alteration to a common plastic cap and placed evenly along the length of the rope. At the ground level, the rope is strung around a pulley at the top of the loop, which, when rotated, runs the rope down into a well where water is captured between the pistons in the pipe. The diameter of the pistons fits snugly within the pipe to contain the water and pull it up through the tube. By simply turning a hand crank at ground level, a user can bring large volumes of water quickly and easily to the surface.

The pump's aboveground components are painted with a sealer, base coat, and top coat, which prevent against corrosion and rust, extending the lifespan of the system as a whole and its individual parts. All the materials used can be found at most marketplaces in the region, making obtaining spare parts and performing maintenance easy. Ideas at Work and RDIC also produce operation and maintenance manuals in Khmer and host training sessions for the operation of the ROVAI pumps at the time of installation.

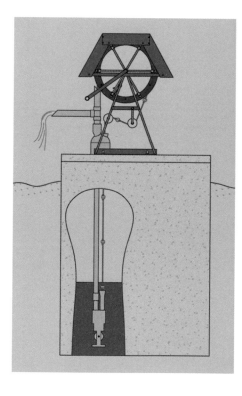

designers:
Ideas at Work, Resource Development International–Cambodia (RDIC)

geographical implementation/ market/availability:
Cambodia, on project basis through Ideas at Work or RDIC

status:
Limited distribution

price:
$90–$300

websites:
www.ideas-at-work.org
www.rdic.org

SinkPositive

Low-flow toilets are ubiquitous in the USA, but every flush still wastefully uses fresh water on a task that does not require it—refilling the toilet's bowl and tank. SinkPositive saves water by using a toilet's freshwater refill cycle for hand washing, then channeling the dirty sink water into the bowl. The system fits as a lid on most standard toilets. When the toilet flushes normally, the new freshwater is piped up to the sink on top of the lid, which then drains into the bowl. SinkPositive provides a useful, intermediate step between the toilet bowl and new incoming water that saves additional water from being used in a separate sink.

By using an existing water supply (the toilet) for a second use (sink hand-washing), the user saves water and money and reduces waste. The sink automatically runs with the toilet's freshwater refill cycle, so there are no knobs or handles to touch. The immediate flow and convenient location of the running faucet also encourage users to wash their hands

with every flush. Additionally, because the entire system fits squarely on the toilet like a standard lid, SinkPositive saves space. The toilet-top sink can also aid in the early detection of leaks in the toilet's plumbing, since each flush's capacity can be monitored through the faucet flow.

SinkPositive is easily installed; it simply creates a bridge between the bowl refill supply tube (where the water comes into the toilet tank) and the overflow pipe (where the water flows from the tank into the bowl). The refill supply tube is attached to the faucet under the lid, so that fresh water comes in the supply tube and moves directly up to the sink faucet. The sink's drain is then connected to the overflow pipe, so that as sink water flows down the drain, it goes into the bowl. When flushed, waste and bowl water are disposed of as usual.

designer:
Environmental Designworks, LLC
**geographical implementation/
market/availability:**
USA, via website
status:
Consumer product
price:
$109–$119
website:
www.sinkpositive.com

SODIS

An open-source, do-it-yourself technology for solar water disinfection, SODIS uses UVA radiation and the sun's heat to eliminate pathogens that cause diarrhea and other waterborne diseases. The simple technique is ideal for small quantities of water to be used at the household level. All that is needed is a supply of transparent glass or PET plastic bottles and adequate sunlight. Bottles are filled with water and placed under the sun atop the home's roof, if possible on a corrugated iron sheet that reflects the sunlight. The bottles must be left in the sun for six hours at 50 percent cloudiness and two full days at 100 percent cloudiness.

The SODIS method is only effective for water at low turbidity levels (less than 30 NTU). Eawag recommends placing the headlines of a newspaper or a piece of paper with "SODIS" written on it under the bottle. If the letters on the paper are legible looking from the top to the bottom of the standing bottle in the shade, the water's turbidity is low enough for the technique to be effective.

System rather than product, SODIS gives citizens the tools they need to ensure their own water safety with little cost other than the expense of necessary materials. Eawag has aided in the distribution of picture-based instructional manuals to teach the SODIS technique on a global scale since 1995, and the system has been recommended by the World Health Organization as a household water treatment method since 2001.

designer:
Department of Water and Sanitation in Developing Countries (Sandec) at the Swiss Federal Institute of Aquatic Science and Technology (Eawag)

geographical implementation/ market/availability:
Global

status:
DIY

price:
Cost of materials

website:
www.sodis.ch

well-being

Adaptive Eyecare

designer:
 Joshua Silver
**geographical implementation/
market/availability:**
 Global, on project basis
status:
 Limited distribution
price:
 Approx. $10
website:
 www.adaptive-eyecare.com

The World Health Organization estimates that approximately one billion people, including 10 percent of school children, require vision correction but are untreated. Developed by British physicist Joshua Silver, Adaptive Eyecare glasses feature fluid-filled lenses that have the potential to inexpensively and efficiently aid almost everyone in need. In virtually all markets, affordable, adaptable tools for vision correction are a necessity, particularly in developing countries where many children and elderly citizens do not have access to proper vision care. Adaptive Eyecare lenses can easily treat afflictions including presbyopia and myopia and can be successfully prescribed and delivered with little medical training.

In Silver's design, each lens consists of two flexible membranes with liquid between them. The lenses are sealed for water-tightness within a sturdy frame, and the amount of fluid is adjusted to suit the individual's needs: the more fluid, the more the membranes flex, which produces a greater curvature and a stronger prescription. The power of the lenses can be between +6 and -6 diopters, a range that corrects vision for nearly 90 percent of patients. At the time of fitting, the wearer can personally adjust the power of each lens by turning a small device attached to the glasses that controls the flow of fluid between the membranes. After making modifications, the lenses are set, and the ancillary device for adjustment is removed and discarded.

To date the glasses have been distributed in Africa and Asia, at a price point of approximately $10 per pair. Further distribution is planned for Ghana and other African nations, and Silver estimates that the price could decrease with improved technology and manufacturing.

Antivirus

designer:
Hân Pham
other partners/clients/producers:
SP Moulding A/S
**geographical implementation/
market/availability:**
Global
status:
In development
website:
www.yellowone.dk

Accidental contact with contaminated needles accounts for hundreds of thousands of HIV infections and millions of Hepatitis A and B infections annually, primarily due to the unsafe separation of needles from their syringe bases and the subsequent disposal of the needles. Antivirus is a simple, plastic cap that permanently attaches to the top of a standard aluminum soda can and facilitates the safe removal and disposal of needles immediately after they are used. Antivirus's functionality is dependent on its attachment to the empty can, a particularly abundant waste product in areas where safe water is inaccessible and many people rely on soda or bottled beverages. These locations are also some of the same areas where needle-stick injuries are most common.

The polypropylene plastic cap snaps onto the can and is then locked in place permanently. After performing an injection, a user places the syringe's needle tip into the cap's opening. The cap's built-in system safely dislocates the needle and drops it into the container. The large collar and small hole—which is too small for a finger to pass through—further protect users from infection. Each can holds 150 to 400 needles depending on its depth. Additionally, the cap's form is molded with international hazardous-waste and danger graphics, making them non-language-specific and universally understood. Antivirus was an INDEX: AWARD Top Nominee in 2007.

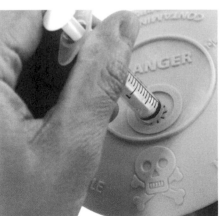

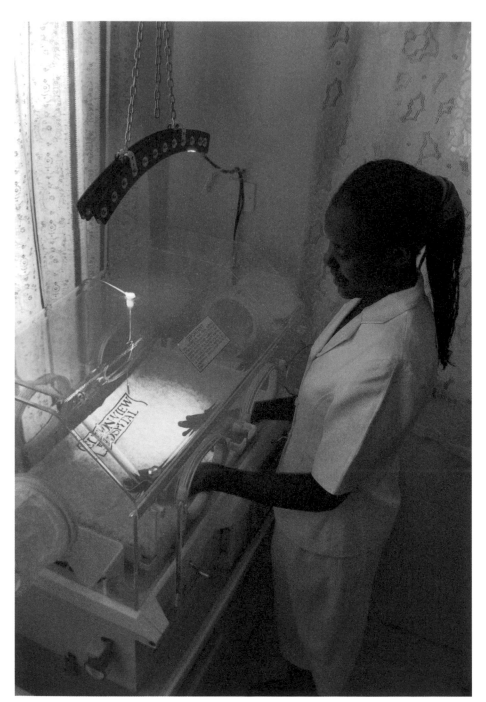

designers:
　　PhotoGenesis Medical,
　　Tackle Design, Inc.
other partners/clients/producers:
　　Duke University, Engineering
　　World Health
geographical implementation/
market/availability:
　　Global, on project basis through
　　PhotoGenesis
status:
　　Limited distribution
price:
　　Approx. $500
website:
　　www.photogenesismedical.com

BlueRay Phototherapy

Infantile jaundice is a condition that develops in the first days of life, when a baby's liver is not mature enough to metabolize bilirubins, molecules that form naturally when the body recycles damaged red blood cells. Each year more than two million infants, primarily in the developing world, are affected by jaundice, the symptoms of which include a yellowish discoloration of the skin. If left untreated, jaundice can damage other organs in the body and lead to kernicterus, a form of brain damage that can cause cerebral palsy and hearing loss. While jaundice is easily reversed in developed countries using a light-based treatment called phototherapy, most devices that perform the treatment are expensive and require frequent maintenance, making them inaccessible to the developing world.

BlueRay Phototherapy provides an affordable, highly effective and safe alternative that is customized to the needs of hospitals and medical professionals in the developing world. At approximately $500 per unit, the phototherapy device is 10 times cheaper than comparable models used in the USA and runs for five years without maintenance. The boomerang-sized BlueRay uses long-lasting LED lights rather than the UV lamps employed in traditional phototherapy devices. The freestanding and portable unit can easily be transported from crib to crib and includes a rechargeable battery that offers 24 hours of uninterrupted power.

The device began as a research initiative in 2006 by Duke University engineering student Vijay Anand. Its development has since become a collaboration between Duke's Engineering World Health and Chuck Messer, Jesse Crossen, Jonathan Kuniholm, and Kevin Webb from Tackle Design, a product design firm based in Durham, North Carolina, that helped significantly lower the tool's manufacturing costs. BlueRay was the winner of the CUREs contest, which provided the team with $100,000 in seed money to establish a nonprofit company, PhotoGenesis Medical, to support the commercialization and further distribution of the product. Two of the largest distributors of medical equipment to the developing world have placed orders, and PhotoGenesis has begun more regular, independent distribution of the devices to facilities in Africa, Asia, and other areas.

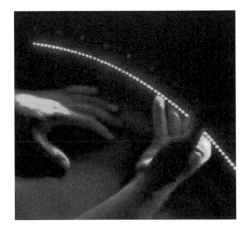

Freedom HIV/AIDS

designer:
ZMQ Software Systems

other partners/clients/producers:
House of Learning, local phone service providers

geographical implementation/ market/availability:
India, by download

status:
Project implemented

price:
Free

website:
www.freedomhivaids.in

Mobile devices have become the most prevalent communications tool worldwide—in developed and developing markets alike. Freedom HIV/AIDS is the first cell-phone-based HIV/AIDS awareness campaign and the world's largest cell-phone-based social initiative. The educational program consists of four mobile phone games: "Safety Cricket," "Ribbon Chase," "The Messenger," and "Quiz with Babu." Each employs a different strategy for HIV/AIDS awareness and education. In "Ribbon Chase," for example, your character is a red AIDS ribbon, and an HIV virus is chasing you around the globe. Different cities ask you for information about HIV/AIDS, and you must deliver it to them in a timely manner in order to escape the virus. The multilevel game gives you five lives to deliver messages worldwide.

Freedom HIV/AIDS was launched on World AIDS Day (December 1) in 2005 by Delhi-based ZMQ Software Systems. In their first phase, the games were available through Reliance Communications, a mobile operator network, and reached 9 million handsets. Since then 42 million users have downloaded the free games directly from their phones through multiple service providers.

The games continue to grow in popularity and have been effective in bringing an urgent public-health campaign to an accessible device through a fun, interactive experience. ZMQ continues to develop new games for an expanded market and has recently reached mobile-phone users in Africa through a service provider that covers Kenya, Malawi, Mozambique, Namibia, Tanzania, and Uganda. Further expansions to Eastern Europe, Latin America, and Southeast Asia are in development, as are new games addressing tuberculosis, malaria, smoking, drugs, and prenatal care.

Pause

HomeHero Fire Extinguisher

The HomeHero Fire Extinguisher is a user-friendly, attractive alternative to the traditional red fire extinguisher, which most consumers find cumbersome and difficult to use. A winner of the 2007 IDEA award from the Industrial Designers Society of America, HomeHero has a molded rubber grip, highly visible safety pin, and trigger on its handle. These features allow the extinguisher to be deployed with just one hand and make it comfortable and easy to operate even in the high-stress moments in which it is required. While most extinguishers are considered eyesores and are kept out of sight, HomeHero's sleek form makes it suitable for more visible display, which means it is more likely to be within arm's reach during an emergency.

HomeHero can also be wirelessly connected to the brand's two-in-one Smoke and Carbon Monoxide Alarm via an accessory Docking Station. When linked to the HomeHero, the alarm alerts the entire house whenever the extinguisher is removed from its base. The system comes with a six-year warranty and an expected life of 12 years and was developed exclusively for The Home Depot.

designer:
Arnell Group, LLC
other partners/clients/producers:
ORANGE WORKS group at
The Home Depot
**geographical implementation/
market/availability:**
USA, via website and
The Home Depot stores
status:
Consumer product
price:
$30
websites:
www.homehero.net
www.homedepot.com

Intel Mobile Clinical Assistant (MCA)

designer:
　Whipsaw, Inc.
other partners/clients/producers:
　Intel Corp., Motion Computing
geographical implementation/ market/availability:
　Global, via dealers including
　Motion Computing, Panasonic,
　and Philips FIMI
status:
　Limited distribution
price:
　$2,199
website:
　www.intel.com

Bringing vital medical information to the point of care, the Intel MCA is a portable computer platform that stores, processes, and organizes patient data. Since 2004 Intel has conducted in-depth user-based research, working with healthcare professionals and analyzing ethnographic research and workflow studies to provide new product offerings that would increase the productivity of high-pressure medical environments. A direct result of this focus, the MCA combines wireless networking for sending and receiving electronic medical records, an integrated digital camera for on-site documentation, and a barcode scanner for use on IV bags and medication bottles to avoid errors in dispensing. Unlike conventional laptop computers, the MCA uses situation-specific software tailored to the needs of both the patient and healthcare provider that can be easily used at the moment care is delivered.

The product, which is currently employed in hospitals worldwide, is lightweight and has a clipboard-like shape and integrated handle, making it easy to carry. Its rugged casing is durable and resistant to spills. In work environments where interruptions are common and details can get lost, the MCA supports the five "rights" of patient care: right patient, right time, right medication, right dosage, and right route. Above all it is a central conduit to ensure accuracy, efficiency, and productivity within the high-stress environment of a clinic, emergency room, or hospital ward.

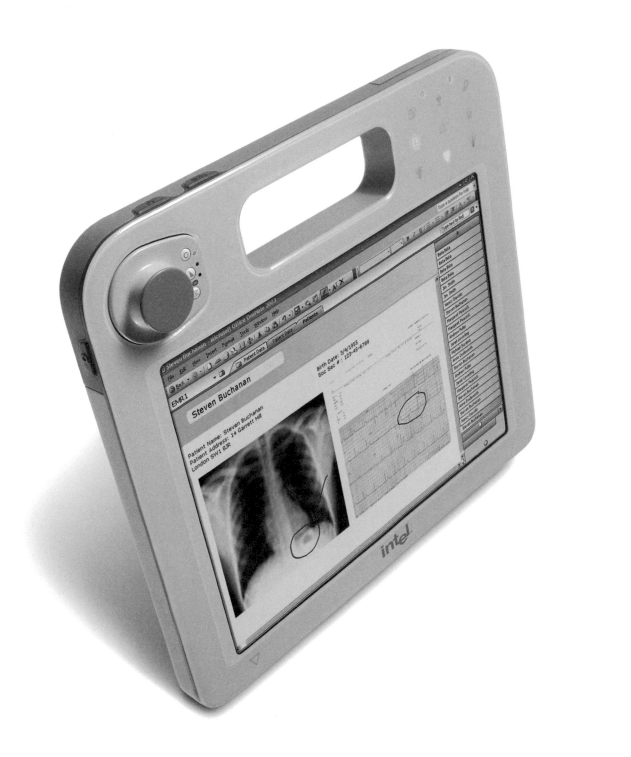

Jaipur Foot

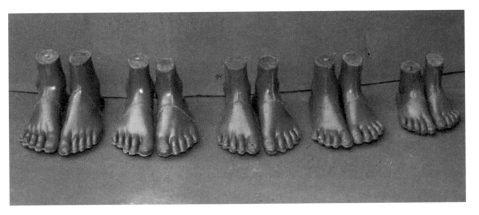

designer:
Bhagwan Mahaveer Viklang
Sahayata Samiti (BMVSS)
**geographical implementation/
market/availability:**
Global, at BMVSS temporary sites
status:
Limited distribution
price:
Approx. $35
website:
www.jaipurfoot.org

The Jaipur Foot, named after the Indian city in which it was first made, is a quick-fit, low-cost prosthesis for landmine victims, amputees, and the physically challenged in the developing world. Created by craftsman Ram Chandra Sharma and orthopedic surgeon Dr. P. K. Sethi, the prosthetic foot is waterproof, flexible along multiple axes, and can be worn with or without shoes to accommodate a range of activities, cultures, and terrains. The production process employs heated high-density polyethylene pipes for the outer socket, which yields a seamless, strong, inert, nontoxic, and biocompatible foot. Its form mirrors that of the human foot as closely as possible. Realistic toes and the ability to flex allow for almost every normal foot movement including dorsiflexion, inversion, eversion, supination, pronation, and axial rotation.

The Jaipur Foot has been used in dozens of countries including Afghanistan, Honduras, India, Nigeria, and Vietnam. The relatively inexpensive prosthetic can be fitted in one visit to a doctor with minimal mechanical adjustments, can be manufactured in a matter of hours, and has a life span of approximately three years. The technology behind the foot takes advantage of traditional craft skills and the abilities of small local producers. BMVSS is a social organization dedicated to improving mobility for the physically challenged. The Jaipur Foot is distributed through the "camp" approach, in which patients are fitted for the prosthetics at temporary sites set up by the organization in areas in need.

The original Jaipur Foot was developed in 1968, and it has been re-engineered and improved in multiple subsequent iterations. Modern tools, new materials, biomechanics, and new production facilities have all led to a superior prosthetic. In countries rife with undiscovered landmines, which cause daily injuries, the Jaipur Foot is a viable and affordable solution for many who suffer from lost mobility. To date it has helped close to one million amputees in countries affected by land mine problems.

Mechanical Advantage Tourniquet (MAT)

designers:
Ewing Design Group,
Cybertech Medical

other partners/clients/producers:
Pyng Medical

**geographical implementation/
market/availability:**
Global, via Pyng Medical and
other dealers

status:
Consumer product

price:
Approx. $40

website:
www.mat-tourniquet.com

The MAT stops blood flow in 10 seconds, requires only one hand to operate, and makes it possible for an injured person to save her own life. The mechanical version of a standard arm tourniquet provides complete circumferential compression, resulting in a quick, safe, and effective occlusion of blood flow. MAT has been used in the dark, in combat, for emergency medical services, under water, and while submersed in mud, grime, oil, and sand.

The design was optimized to be as easy to use as possible in high-stress, emergency scenarios. MAT's strap is held in place with a buckle and tightened with a turnkey, and it can be fastened for effective use in just four easy steps. First, the tourniquet is placed around the injured appendage using the specifically designed grip that facilitates one-handed operation. Next the tourniquet is engaged by fastening the buckle, which clicks audibly into place. Third, the user cinches the band so it fits her appendage snugly. Finally, the turnkey is rotated to tighten the tourniquet, thereby safely occluding blood flow with even pressure around the appendage. The MAT is removed simply by pushing the release tab or lifting the buckle. The object is self-explanatory and does not require an instruction manual or training.

In the case of the MAT, the enhancement of a design by mechanical components has measurably increased the efficacy of a device used in the gravest of moments. Multiple independent military medical tests have proven the MAT to be the fastest, most effective, and easiest-to-use of all tourniquets.

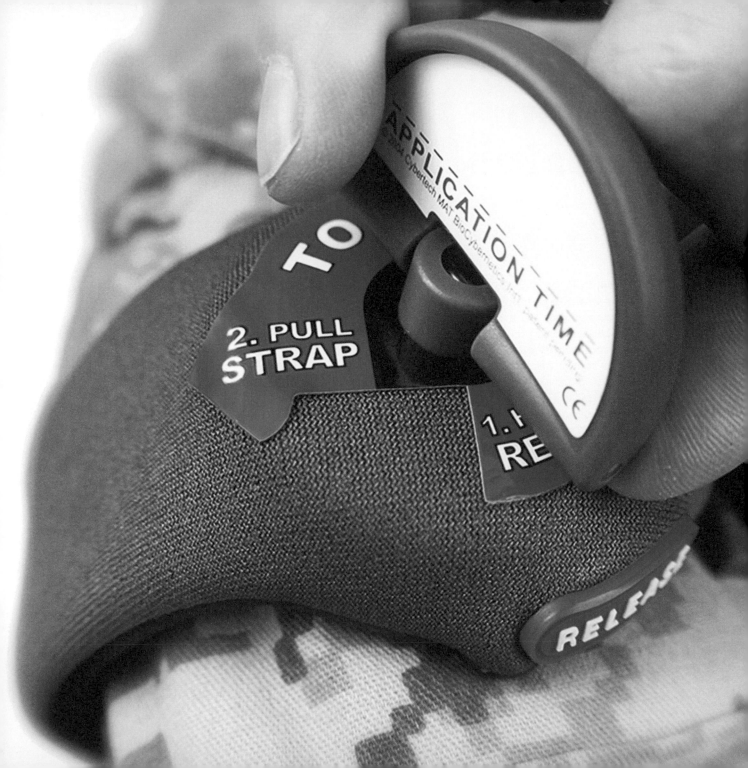

NYC Condom Campaign

Fuseproject's designs for the packaging, dispenser, and campaign branding of the NYC Condom make safe sex sexy, while also demonstrating that design can have tangible social impacts. The New York City Health Department's initiative to distribute free condoms as an effective measure against HIV infections and unwanted pregnancies was made personal, friendly, and successful through the design strategy that destigmatizes the discussion of safe sex. "Good design can help bring condoms out of the closet," states Yves Behar, founder of fuseproject. "The brand's friendly design and the dispenser's approachable shape convey openness and acceptance. They say condoms are nothing to be embarrassed about."

The iconic design for the NYC Condom packaging and dispenser helped the public-health campaign achieve two goals: raise the awareness and use of the condoms by its citizens, and motivate the implementation of the dispensers by businesses and organizations throughout the city. Within the first 10 months of the program, distribution of free condoms increased from 10 million to 30 million.

The design of the dispenser was inspired by the warped shape a condom leaves on the surface of a leather wallet, further turning the taboo into the beautiful. Even the fonts used, a sans serif Gotham and Gotham Rounded, exude friendliness, youth, and familiarity, as the typeface's roots can be traced back to signs on New York buildings in the 1930s. The dispensers, the primary distribution system for the condoms, have been mounted on walls in more than 200 city venues ranging from bodegas and bars to coffee shops and clothing stores.

"The NYC Condom has shown us what a sexy brand can do for safer sex," affirms Dr. Monica Sweeney, the Health Department's Assistant Commissioner for HIV Prevention and Control, perfectly articulating design's potential to increase the effectiveness of public health and other social programs in personal and sustainable ways.

designer:
  fuseproject
other partners/clients/producers:
  New York City Department of
  Health and Mental Hygiene
**geographical implementation/
market/availability:**
  New York City, via Health
  Department and citywide
  dispensers
status:
  Project implemented
price:
  Free
websites:
  www.fuseproject.com
  www.nyc.gov/condoms

OneTouch UltraMini Blood Glucose Meter

For diabetics, monitoring glucose levels multiple times throughout the day is the key to controlling the disease and maintaining a suitable diet and ongoing health. Personal glucose meters, however, can be frustrating to carry, difficult to read, and impersonal to use. The OneTouch UltraMini Blood Glucose Meter is affordable, small, and simple, delivering readings in five seconds and in three easy steps. To begin the testing process, which is more efficient than that of other meters, insert a test strip into the port and produce a drop of blood using the lancing device. Apply the blood to the testing strip and press a button on the meter. The monitor will count down the seconds, from five to one, at which point the blood glucose level, along with unit of measure, date, and time, will be displayed on the screen. The meter can store up to 50 test results for further diagnostics. Additionally, unlike other meters, the UltraMini can be used on testing sites other than the finger, including the forearm and palm, where there are fewer nerve endings.

The product works with One-Touch Ultra's test strips, which are covered by more health plans than any other test strip, resulting in a potential average savings of $240 per year. The sleek meter, which is about 3 inches (7.6 cm) in length, comes in six vibrant colors, bringing a personalized touch to an otherwise sterile experience. The UltraMini also comes with Simple Start, an educational booklet that provides information about glucose and meal management for diabetics.

designers:
   Johnson & Johnson, LifeScan, Inc.
**geographical implementation/
market/availability:**
   USA, via website and dealers
status:
   Consumer product
price:
   Approx. $20, plus test strips
website:
   www.onetouchdiabetes.com/
   ultramini

Spider Boot

designer:
GadShaananDESIGN

other partners/clients/producers:
Med-Eng Systems, Inc.,
a subsidiary of Allen-Vanguard
CORP

**geographical implementation/
market/availability:**
Global, via Allen-Vanguard

status:
Limited distribution

websites:
www.med-eng.com
www.gadshaanandesign.com

The Spider Boot foot protection system is a revolutionary design that protects a deminer's feet and legs against shock waves from antipersonnel blast mines. There are an estimated 70 to 110 million land mines buried in more than 60 countries, and they kill or injure an average of 100 people daily. The Spider Boot can be worn during reconnaissance, detection, and victim assistance operations to ensure the safe discovery and removal of land mines.

In principle, the boot is quite simple: The user straps his combat shoes into the one-size-fits-all platform, which distances the foot from the source of the potential blast. Through the product's research process, designers discovered that most land-mine casualties occur not because of shrapnel, but due to shock waves that emanate from directly underneath the victim's leg. The boot disperses the blast energy and fragments away from the foot using its platform and four stilts. To further reduce energy absorption, the stilts break away from the platform upon impact.

The Spider Boot, designed for Med-Eng Systems, a subsidiary of Allen-Vanguard, has been exhibited at The Museum of Modern Art, New York. Med-Eng is an international leader in the production of bomb-protection gear and distributes directly to the United Nations and military outfits worldwide. The system has proven to provide four to five times the protection of conventional mine boots.

StarSight Project

The StarSight street lighting system is a solar-powered, disaster-proof, networked infrastructure that can deliver reliable lighting and wireless capabilities to large cities and the rural developing world. Its technology bypasses conventional power and telecommunication grids to provide increased connectivity for emerging economies, disaster-struck locations, and urban centers. Reliable street lighting reduces local crime, extends working hours, and enhances public safety. In developing countries, it allows for new enterprises to emerge and is viewed positively by potential investors.

The StarSight system communicates directly to a Network Operating Center (NOC) that controls when the lights are turned on and off and monitors maintenance requirements. It is also CCTV-enabled to communicate with emergency dispatchers and work as a disaster communications system. The system can withstand Category Three hurricanes and network wirelessly off the phone grid when communication is most needed.

Each of the system's lights is made from die-cast aluminum and highly lucent, toughened glass and is coated in fluorocarbon powder for protection against dirt and weathering. The units employ energy-efficient LEDs and battery and solar panels for energy harvesting and storage. The LED lights are lower energy, more durable, and longer lasting than conventional lights, and since they range from 30 to 120 watts, they are appropriate for all urban street lighting requirements. The units are also linked to StarSight's wireless technologies for communication with the NOC.

StarSight is optimized for low capital expenditures: It requires no excavation for the installation of underground cables and has low operational costs and a minimal energy budget. The system can also be used to generate income through commercial exploitation of its wireless Internet access, or in the developing

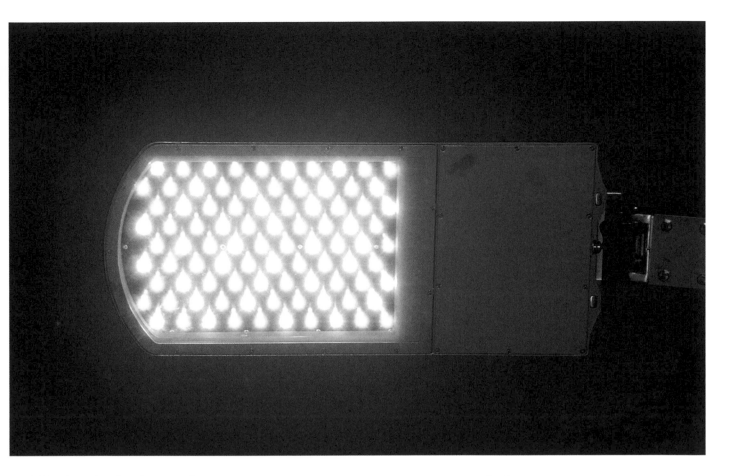

world by the sale of carbon credits through the United Nations' Clean Development Mechanism.

The StarSight system is currently in use in locations including Cameroon, Côte d'Ivoire, the Republic of the Congo, and Istanbul, where it serves as both the city's commercial wireless Internet network and local earthquake emergency communications system.

designer:
StarSight International
other partners/clients/producers:
Kolam Partnership, Ltd.
geographical implementation/ market/availability:
Global, on project basis for municipal and civic installations
status:
Limited distribution
website:
www.starsightproject.com

Stop Thief Anti-Theft Furniture

designer:
Design Against Crime
other partners/clients/producers:
Central Saint Martins College
of Art and Design at University
of the Arts London
status:
Concept
website:
www.designagainstcrime.com

Design Against Crime is a socially responsive, practice-led research center at Central Saint Martins College of Art and Design at University of the Arts London. Its research projects combine strategies for personal and community safety with traditionally designed objects and systems. One such project, Stop Thief Anti-Theft Furniture, illustrates the research center's tenet that "secure design should not look criminal," and combines personal security elements with classic and comfortable design

The Stop Thief Ply Chair and Stop Thief Bentwood Chair are interpretations of Arne Jacobsen's iconic Series 7 chair and Michael Thonet's bentwood designs. Each chair features two slots on which the user can hang a purse or other personal belongings while seated. This keeps the property safe and the floor clear of obstructions. The project is a unique example of incremental design, which makes small changes to the designs and aesthetics of already accepted objects to elevate the original item's function

to a more socially responsible level. While many may recognize Jacobsen's chair as a modernist icon, the small slits that Design Against Crime has cut into the seats are a minor edit that transforms the object into a high-impact tool for public safety.

Subtle Safety Ring

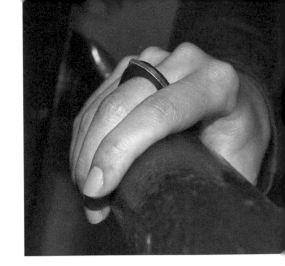

The Subtle Safety Ring is both a beautiful piece of jewelry and a reminder to women to make safe choices. Its unique, asymmetrical shape comes to a point on one side, giving the wearer a sense of security and serving to keep self-defense on her mind. In the same way that women are encouraged to carry their keys between their fingers while walking home, the ring imparts a feeling of safety rather than serving as an aggressive weapon. An earlier version of the ring could be worn across three fingers, while RedStart's current design is a three-tiered, stainless-steel, red acrylic ring for one finger.

The ring was part of The Museum of Modern Art's exhibition *SAFE: Design Takes on Risk* in 2005. While Subtle Safety is not intended for violent use, its form is a constant visual cue that prompts women to take personal safety into their own hands.

designer:
    RedStart Design
geographical implementation/ market/availability:
    Global, via website
status:
    Consumer product
price:
    $78
website:
    www.redstartdesign.com

Target Pharmacy Bottle

With extremely technical language cramped into a small space, prescription bottle labels can be daunting and confusing to read. Though taking medicine on time and in the dose prescribed is essential to its efficacy, according to a recent poll conducted for Target, 60 percent of prescription-drug users have taken medication incorrectly. To address the less than stellar design of its prescription bottles, the big-box retailer turned to graphic designer Deborah Adler, whose thesis project at the School of Visual Arts was an innovative and improved way to package medication. Adler and Target branded and refined the concept, and the result offers a new experience in filling and taking prescription medication that is more user-friendly for both pharmacists and patients.

While traditional prescription bottles are visually confusing, the Target Pharmacy bottle relies on reconceptualized ways to communicate with the patient, from an easy-to-read label to color indicators

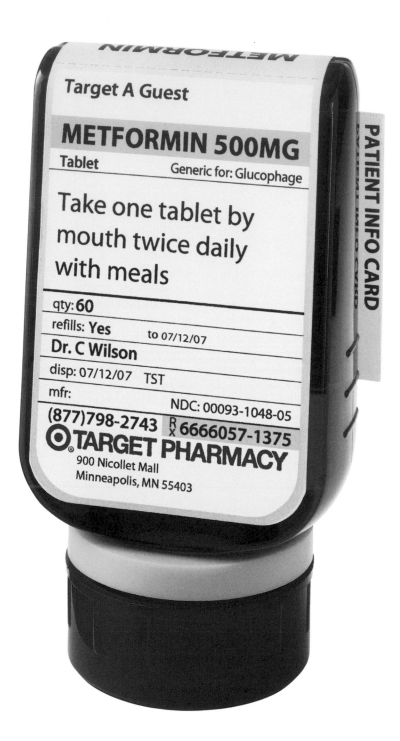

Target A Guest

METFORMIN 500MG

Tablet   Generic for: Glucophage

Take one tablet by mouth twice daily with meals

qty: **60**

refills: **Yes**   to 07/12/07

Dr. C Wilson

disp: 07/12/07   TST

mfr:

NDC: 00093-1048-05

(877)798-2743   Rx 6666057-1375

⊙ **TARGET PHARMACY**
900 Nicollet Mall
Minneapolis, MN 55403

PATIENT INFO CARD

designer:
Deborah Adler
other partners/clients/producers:
Target Corporation
geographical implementation/ market/availability:
USA, at Target stores
status:
Consumer product
website:
www.target.com

and health information pamphlets. Standard industry bottles suffer from inconsistent labeling, neutral colors that hinder rather than help, confusing number placement, a curved, slender shape that makes labels hard to read, and the use of tiny type. Adler's solution puts function over form, combining smart elements for quick and easy comprehension. The new bottle's shape is easy to grip. Its large, flat face allows for expanded labels with bigger, clearer fonts for better readability. A reorganization of basic information puts drug name and prescribing instructions at the top of both the label and the bottle so that the most crucial information may be read from above, while a removable information card providing additional instructions and medication details tucks securely into the bottle's back sleeve. Color-coded rings help clearly identify each person's medicine in multipatient homes, and newly designed icons make recommendations such as, "take on an empty stomach," clearer.

Adler was inspired to redesign the bottle when her grandmother accidentally ingested pills prescribed for her grandfather. After that experience, Adler realized not only the aesthetic disadvantages but also the physical dangers of traditional prescription bottles. The new bottle has been used by Target pharmacies nationwide since 2005.

Vaccine Patch – Transcutaneous Immunization (TCI)

Given that many people have a fear of needles and that every injection—without exception—must be dependable and sterile, delivering immunizations by the standard means, a shot in the arm, can be problematic. Intercell's TCI patch is a solution to the problems of that method, providing a needle-free alternative to injected immunizations. When applied to the skin, the needleless vaccine patch cues the body's immune response that is required for disease protection. The TCI patch delivers immune stimulants known as adjuvants through the skin's surface to the Langerhan cells, which are major elements of the immune system. As the Langerhan cells are activated by the presence of these stimulants, they take in the vaccine antigen and migrate to the regional draining lymph nodes. There, the body responds and becomes effectively immunized.

The patch's advantages over traditional injections are numerous, from its easy, needle-free, sterile administration to its accessible dis-tribution, stability at a wider range of temperatures, and applicability within both the developed and developing world. IDEO integrated a mail-out packaging system that makes the immunization process both full-service and self-service for patients and doctors. The patch's design considers the user first, prioritizing patient usability and comfort.

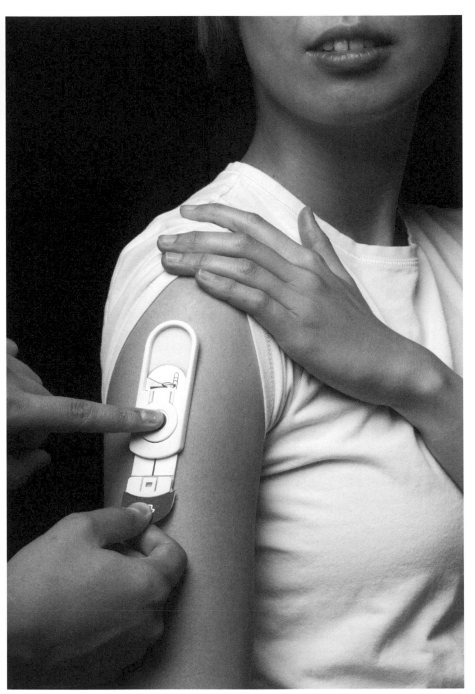

designer:
 IDEO
other partners/clients/producers:
 Iomai, now part of Intercell
**geographical implementation/
market/availability:**
 Global, to medical professionals
 through Intercell
status:
 Limited distribution
website:
 www.intercell.com

energy

Air X

designer:
Southwest Windpower
**geographical implementation/
market/availability:**
Global, via dealers
status:
Consumer product
price:
$700–$900
website:
www.windenergy.com

The Air X is the world's top-selling small wind turbine. Suitable for residential or commercial applications, the entry-level turbine gathers the wind's power and stores it in a battery pack, which can then power small electronics. Its microprocessor-based technology, efficient battery charging, and ability to monitor wind conditions for optimal power generation set it apart from comparable products and make it a low-cost and accessible means to harness renewable energy. Air X is most appropriate to provide power for small appliances such as TVs, radios, or lights, though many users add it to an existing power system to reduce or eliminate dependence on a backup generator. The compact turbine weighs only 13 pounds (6 kg), with a rotor diameter of just 46 inches (1.15 m). It requires a start-up wind speed of 8 miles per hour (3.5 m/s), and can produce up to 38 kWh of power per month at an average wind speed of 12 miles per hour (5.4 m/s).

With the Air X, Southwest Wind-power has improved upon its previous turbine models by incorporating microprocessors that ensure steady, increased performance, improved battery charging capability, and quieter operation. The turbine self-regulates the rate and amount of power collected and stored by tracking the power of the wind. Blade rotation speed can be controlled to eliminate noise without sacrificing efficiency. The battery monitor ensures the most effective charge possible.

Because the entire system only employs two moving parts (which make up the rotating blade and alternator system), maintenance is minimal. Air X's low cost, built-in, controlled technologies make it ideal for the developing world, off-the-grid homes, telecommunication towers, and monitoring stations. To date, Air X has the best cost-per-watt value of any wind turbine.

BoGo Light

SunNight Solar's buy-one-give-one BoGo Lights are rugged, solar powered flashlights that use efficient LED bulbs, which last for an average of 100,000 hours, compared to a traditional incandescent bulb's 100 hours. The flashlight has a built-in solar panel, which harnesses the sun's rays and stores the energy in rechargeable batteries, which can provide six to eight continuous hours of light on a full charge. There are two models of the light: the original SL-1 and the heightened SL-2, which comes fully equipped with three settings (low, medium, and high), a printed circuit board, an added boost converter, and an additional transistor per LED.

While the solar flashlight is nothing new, thanks to SunNight Solar's enterprising BoGo business model, the SL-1 and SL-2 are much more than environmentally conscious ways to navigate the dark. When a light is purchased through the company's website or a retail outlet, another is donated to a person in need through a nonprofit partner of the buyer's choosing. These partners include schools in the USA, troops in Afghanistan and Iraq, and international development and health groups. To date, the program has successfully provided light to thousands of people in the developing world, enabling nighttime education and productivity in locations without access to reliable electricity. Along with the flashlight, SunNight Solar also provides $1 per light to nonprofit partners to offset associated distribution costs. BoGo's combination of retail marketability and philanthropy is a forward-thinking business practice that bridges markets through product design.

designer:
    SunNight Solar
geographical implementation/
market/availability:
    Global, via website
status:
    Consumer product
price:
    $39–$49
website:
    www.bogolight.com

Club WATT

The Sustainable Dance Club began as a sold-out, one-time party in October 2005 but has evolved into a company that operates a brick-and-mortar nightlife venue that is powered every evening by the kinetic energy created by dancing. Club WATT opened on September 4, 2008, in Rotterdam, The Netherlands, after close to two years of design and technological development by Sustainable Dance Club (SDC), Dutch sustainable innovation firm Enviu, and design studio Döll, in collaboration with other institutional and educational partners.

The technology behind Club WATT is a piezoelectric dance floor that converts the movement of a dancing crowd into electricity that powers the venue. The club's DJ along with its attendees are challenged to reach the maximum energy level possible, which is represented through lights and graphics in the venue, creating an awareness of the power of personal energy in a social and fun environment. Every person in the club is able to produce 2 to 20 watts, depending on weight and activity level. The harvested energy is fed back into the club's electrical system to power speakers, lights, and more. Using human motion as the energy source yields an estimated 30 percent reduction in overall electricity usage, 50 percent less carbon dioxide emissions, 50 percent less waste production, and 50 percent less water usage. The energy captured also powers LED light displays embedded in the floor itself, which glow brighter and in more vibrant colors based on the amount of energy being harvested. In addition

designers:
   Sustainable Dance Club (SDC), Döll, Enviu
other partners/clients/ producers:
   Cultural Development (The Netherlands), Rotterdam Climate Initiative, Studio Roosegaarde, Delft University of Technology, Eindhoven Technical University
geographical implementation/ market/availability:
   Rotterdam, The Netherlands
status:
   Project implemented
website:
   www.sustainabledanceclub.com

to the energy-producing dance floor, a system on Club WATT's roof catches rainwater that is then used in the restrooms, where there are also waterless urinals.

SDC continues to work to expand its product offerings and implement the piezoelectric floors in additional locations. The company's technologies seamlessly integrate energy-generating systems into everyday life without disrupting existing social habits. Club WATT is a great example of sustainability that is profitable, convenient and innovative, and that brings environmental awareness to contemporary cultural experiences.

Cyclean

designer:
  Alex Gadsden
status:
  Concept
website:
  www.cyclean.biz

Though it is still in development, the Cyclean pedal-powered washing machine has the potential to bring innovation to many through an ingenious application of simple technology. The do-it-yourself, open-source design for the Cyclean uses a spinning bicycle wheel to rotate the drum of a deconstructed washing machine. UK-based Alex Gadsden, who is not a formally trained designer, began tinkering with old washing machine parts after visiting a local junkyard that was teeming with piles of wasted household appliances. The result of his subsequent backyard experiments combines personal fitness with a way to launder clothes using renewable energy.

The mechanics of Cyclean are relatively simple. A washing machine's drum and shocks (the cylindrical vessel that holds the clothes and the mechanism in which it spins) sit within a simple frame made by the user from basic materials such as wood or metal. A wheel from a wheelbarrow is connected to the back of this configuration using a universal joint. The wheelbarrow wheel is then linked to the rear tire of the bicycle with a belt running around both wheels' circumferences. The bike, attached to the frame, is raised slightly so there is no direct contact between tire and ground. When the user pedals, the bike's wheels turn and the rear tire rotates the wheelbarrow wheel, which then spins the washer drum.

In developing a way to turn pedal power into usable energy, Cyclean could have global implications that extend far beyond its grassroots beginnings. Gadsden explains, "This could help many people in developing nations conserve water, and of course, get fit." He intends to make available online full construction plans for the Cyclean, along with a solar-powered shower he is developing. The current Cyclean prototype has been used for local demonstrations, in a family household, and for press and television appearances.

DIY Biodiesel and Straight Vegetable Oil (SVO) Fuel

geographical implementation/ market/availability:
   Global
status:
   DIY
price:
   Cost of materials
websites:
   Resources at
   www.biodieselcommunity.org
   www.greasecar.com
   www.frybrid.com

Biodiesel, as the name implies, is an organically derived alternative to petroleum-based diesel fuel. It is traditionally made from vegetable oil through a process called transesterification, which separates the glycerin from the oil and leaves behind methyl esters, or biodiesel, which has similar properties to petrodiesel. Most diesel engines can also be converted to run off of pure vegetable oil or waste vegetable oil that has not yet been made into biodiesel. While biodiesel is environmentally cleaner, it is not as widely available as traditional diesel fuel.

Until the day that biodiesel is readily available at all gas stations, there are do-it-yourself options to both make the fuel and convert your car to run on biodiesel's main ingredient, vegetable oil. There are many great resources, both in print and online, that can help you make the transition safely and affordably, but here is the quick-and-dirty version:

1. Know the differences.
You will need to understand the three types of fuel for diesel engines and their different purposes and properties before embarking. Petroleum diesel is the "regular" diesel found at gas stations and what most large trucks use. This is the fuel for which diesel engines were designed. It is not biologically derived, but it performs better than biodiesel in cold weather. Biodiesel is a nonpetroleum version of diesel that has been chemically modified to have properties similar to petrodiesel's and is generally mixed with some quantity of that fuel. It comes in different grades that indicate the percentage of biodiesel within the bio-petroleum mix. For example, biodiesel rated B20 (a common mixture used at truck stops) contains 20 percent biodiesel and 80 percent petrodiesel, while B99 and B100 are the purest versions of biodiesel but are less widely available. Lastly, with a few modifications, diesel engines can run on straight vegetable oil (SVO), which can be either off-the-shelf virgin oil or waste vegetable oil. SVO, while perhaps the purest of all the options, turns to gel in low temperatures.

2. Get a diesel car.
You cannot run a car on any of these fuels if you do not have a diesel engine.

3. Fill up with biodiesel.
Scout local biodiesel pumping stations or distributors and purchase your fuel from them. They will likely sell B20, but in some cities and states you may find B99. There are also resources for making your own biodiesel at home using vegetable oil, methane, and lye. Making your own through transesterification requires a chemical understanding of the separation process, as well as clean and safe equipment. The basics of the process are outlined at the end of these instructions. If you want to convert your car's diesel engine to run off of SVO instead, continue to the next steps.

4. Find your source of vegetable oil.
Your two options for SVO are waste oil and off-the-shelf oil like corn or canola. While off-the-shelf oil is easy to find, it can be expensive; however, a low-grade canola oil will suffice. For waste vegetable oil, contact local restaurants, which have large quantities of used oil from fryers, and negotiate with them regarding its disposal. Establishments may be willing to give the oil to you for free. Some cities like San Francisco have networks for finding free waste vegetable oil.

5. Find the appropriate conversion kit.
In order to run your car on either type of SVO, you will need to perform some minor changes to your existing diesel engine using a conversion kit, which can be ordered from various dealers. Kits can range from $600 to $4,000, depending on your car and the conversion system. It is best to do some research on your specific car brand, model, and year, and to pose questions to online forums regarding which kit will work best. Good sources include www.greasecar.com and www.frybrid.com.

6. Install your conversion kit.
The safest bet for installing your kit is to find a mechanic with experience in performing such conversions. For some vehicles, you are effectively voiding any warranties by converting your car, so a skilled mechanic can help to ensure safe installation.

If you are feeling adventurous and want to go it alone, here are a few systems you will need to understand and possibly install:
- Second tank: Most kits include the addition of a second and separate fuel tank to hold only SVO, separate from biodiesel or petrodiesel. Because SVO has different properties and gel-point temperatures than the more standard fuels, it is best to separate the tanks and use them in isolation. Most kits call for the SVO tank to be placed in the trunk of the car.
- SVO-safe hoses for the fuel system: Some older cars' rubber hoses and seals can break down over time with SVO. Many conversion kits include SVO-safe parts to ensure the long life of your hose, tank, and seal systems.
- Heating system: SVO gels at a higher temperature than biodiesel and petrodiesel, which means it does not perform well in cold weather, so it is important to keep it warm. Most conversion kits include a heating component to warm the SVO before it is pumped into the fuel system. A common configuration includes a heater that siphons heat from the radiator directly into the SVO tank.

7. Filter the SVO and fill up!
If you are using waste vegetable oil, you can strain it with a large-mesh coffee filter or simple strainer before using it. The goal is to remove visible leftover food particles. If you are using off-the-shelf oil, you can pour it directly into the tank.

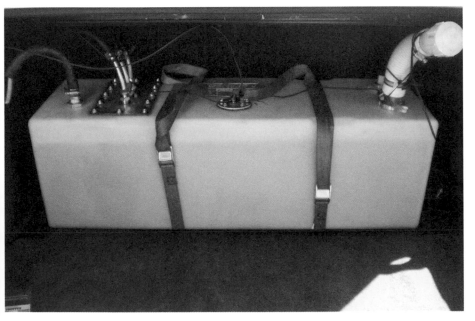

Recipes for homemade biodiesel (for nonconverted engines):

Biodiesel can be made for diesel engines that have not been modified to run on SVO. The fuel can be used interchangeably with petrodiesel or in combination with it. Through the transesterification process, the oil is thinned into fatty acid methyl ester, a form closer to the biodiesel available at the pump.

There are many recipes and variations on the process, but the principles remain the same throughout. If waste vegetable oil is being used, debris and other particles should be filtered. The oil is heated to 130 to 135 °F (54 to 57 °C) while lye and methanol are combined in a separate container. The hot oil is slowly added to the lye and methanol, then the mixture is set aside. It will separate into a layer of glycerin, which will coagulate at the bottom, and biodiesel, which will rise to the top. Once the mixture has cooled, the top layer of biodiesel can be poured directly into a fuel tank. For more recipes and tips, visit the resource center at www.biodiesel-community.org.

EnerJar

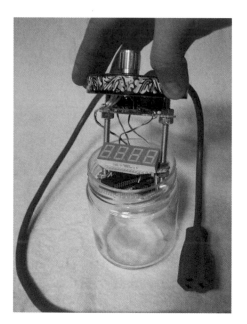

Designed by two third-year students at Washington University in St. Louis, EnerJar is a homemade device that measures the power used by household appliances. Basic electrical equipment and some technical skills are needed to construct the EnerJar (soldering and electrical experience are advantageous). The system consists of a circuit board, potentiometer (which controls and adjusts voltage), LED display, microchip, and standard power cord, all housed within a jar.

The EnerJar assists users in taking the first step toward energy efficiency—awareness. The tool sits between a wall outlet and a household device such as a lamp, laptop, or television, calling attention to the appliance's electricity consumption by displaying the watts of power it is using on a bright LED screen.

For full building instructions and troubleshooting, visit the EnerJar website, where the open-source design is available for free. While the designers are correcting some of EnerJar's safety issues, they continue to work toward the mass production of both the product and kits for its parts, though the open-source model has been successful thus far. EnerJar won the 2008 Greener Gadgets Design Competition hosted by industrial-design website Core77.com.

designers:
    Zach Dwiel, Matt Meshulam
other partners/clients/producers:
    Greener Gadgets Design
    Competition
**geographical implementation/
market/availability:**
    Global
status:
    DIY
price:
    Cost of materials
website:
    www.enerjar.net

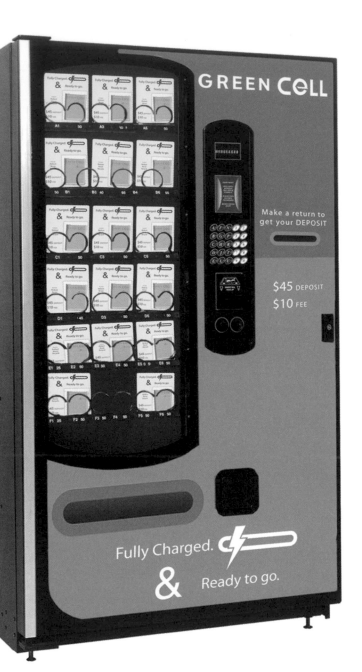

Green Cell

designer:
Rich, Brilliant, Willing
other partners/clients/producers:
Greener Gadgets Design
Competition
**geographical implementation/
market/availability:**
Global
status:
Concept
website:
www.richbrilliantwilling.com

Consumer dependence on the segmented electronics industry results in proprietary, device-specific batteries, plugs, adaptors, and more, which create clutter and inefficiency on a large scale. The argument for a universal battery is obvious, marketable, and—above all—environmentally and socially responsible. For the 2008 Greener Gadgets Design Competition, Theo Richardson, Charles Brill, and Alex Williams of design firm Rich, Brilliant, Willing debuted Green Cell, a forward-thinking concept that provides a unified system for the creation, dispensing, recycling, and disposal of a universal battery for small electronic devices.

The full-service system centers on accessible vending machines through which users may purchase a standard battery for $10, along with a $45 deposit, that would power everything from a BlackBerry to an iPod. The battery would be charged at home or at public charging stations and, when fully used, returned to and recycled at the same vending machines, where the customer would receive back his deposit. The concept offers a solution to two major electronic and environmental problems: creating a standardized format for all devices and implementing an infrastructure to recycle a large quantity of the same thing, rather than the current system that handles small quantities of many things. The concept is simultaneously a creative business model, progressive environmental initiative, and plain good sense.

GROW

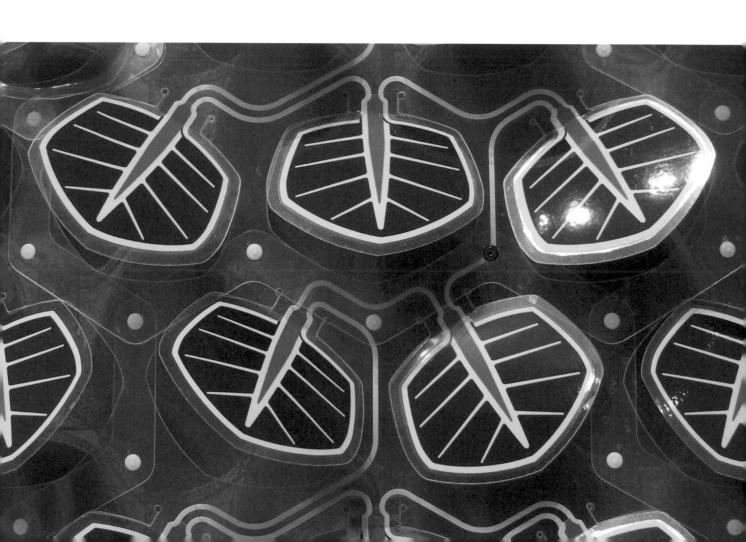

designer:
    Sustainably Minded Interactive
    Technology (SMIT)
other partners/clients/producers:
    Carl Stahl DécorCable,
    PowerFilm, Inc.
geographical implementation/
market/availability:
    Global
status:
    In development
website:
    www.s-m-i-t.com

In a new approach to solar and wind power, design group SMIT has developed two iterations of GROW, a hybrid energy delivery device that, in form, resembles ivy growing on the side of a building. GROW.1 and GROW.2 are the results of a collaboration between siblings Teresita and Samuel Cochran during the former's graduate studies in the Interactive Telecommunications Program at New York University and the latter's undergraduate studies at Pratt Institute. In GROW.1, the original embodiment of the GROW concept, leaflike solar panels harvest the sun's rays, while their collective fluttering harnesses wind power using a series of piezoelectric generators on the underside of each leaf. GROW.2 is a solar-only, residential application built on top of a stainless-steel mesh system. It will soon be available for home use in the form of a 4-by-8-foot (1.2-by-2.4-m) modular panel that can be easily integrated into the exteriors of multiple types of buildings. The photovoltaic leaves are made of 100 percent recyclable polyethylene and can be produced in a variety of colors and opacities.

SMIT's approach is unique in its thoughtful combination of science, art, and sustainability in a single marketable product. Combining cutting-edge, thin photovoltaics and piezoelectric technology in a system that is adaptable to varying building styles and climates, GROW represents a new model for high-tech, accessible, green energy harvesting.

HYmini

What do you get when you combine a hybrid energy device with technology that can fit in the palm of your hand? The HYmini, a compact universal charger that harnesses energy from both green and traditional sources. Drawing power from a conventional 100- to 220-volt wall plug charge, a computer USB connection, attachable miniSOLAR panels also available from MINIWIZ, or its built-in supplemental wind turbine, HYmini can charge almost all 5-volt devices, including cell phones, cameras, and mp3 players.

While other portable chargers rely on a single source of green power, the creators of HYmini were realistic in understanding their customers' desire also to use the device with traditional electricity. This option makes the charger unique, but its most unusual and groundbreaking feature is its supplemental wind turbine. The turbine's 65 mA generator harnesses wind at speeds between 9 and 40 miles per hour (14.5 to 65 km/h), and will automatically shut off if gusts exceed that speed. A built-in light lets the user know when the turbine is charging the internal battery pack. Able to be strapped to a bag or bicycle, the sleek and weatherproof HYmini is a viable option for power on the go.

designer:
MINIWIZ Sustainable Energy Dev., Ltd.
geographical implementation/ market/availability:
Global, via website and dealers
status:
Consumer product
price:
$49.99
website:
www.hymini.com

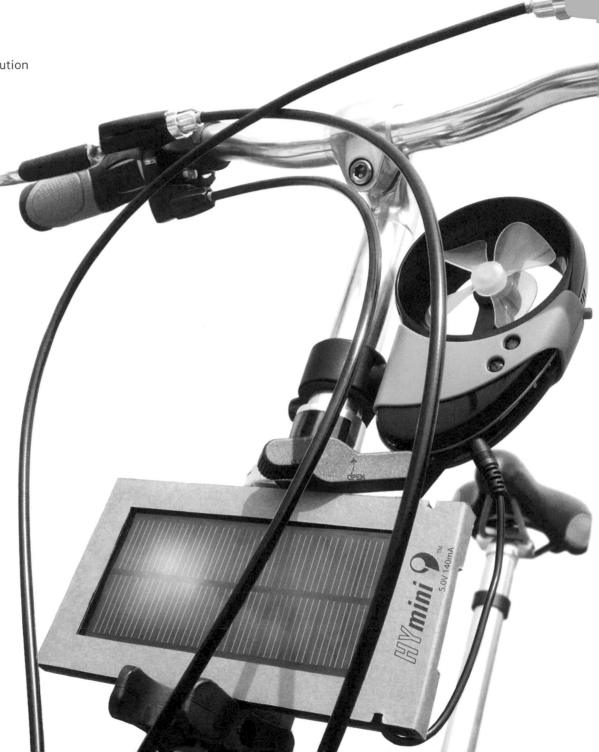

M2E Technology

Based on the assertion that the most renewable energy is that which can be derived from human motion, M2E has developed a technology that turns human kinetics into a viable energy source for personal electronics. While the technology has thus far been implemented only in small case studies for the US Army, the implications are far reaching and could mean the end of chargers for cell phones and other electronic devices.

Large amounts of human motion have been gathered and converted into power in other contexts (see Club WATT, p. 124), but M2E's technology converts even the most minor movements into usable quantities of energy. The company's microgenerator can stay fully charged from a motion as slight as a jostling or vibration, which has obvious applications for the gadgets we carry on a daily basis. Power is generated using motion-activated electromagnetic fields that harvest kinetic energy, convert it to electrical energy, and store that energy for later use. M2E estimates

that this technology, which is rooted in a fundamental change in magnetic architecture, could increase power output by 300 to 700 percent compared to existing configurations.

The development of M2E's technology represents a paradigm shift in energy generation and has widespread benefits for many demographics. For the military, M2E's kinetic energy yields increased mobility, durability, and versatility in combat scenarios, while for consumers, its convenience means less time worrying about waning batteries. Because the charger can be easily integrated into current consumer products and uses basic existing materials, manufacturers will benefit from its easy compatibility and construction. Currently M2E holds the global exclusive license for the technology and its applications. In the coming years the company plans to further refine and develop it for specific and expanded consumer and institutional applications.

designer:
Motion 2 Energy Power, Inc. (M2E)
other partners/clients/producers:
Idaho National Laboratory,
Massachusetts Institute of
Technology (MIT), US Military
**geographical implementation/
market/availability:**
Global, to US military only
status:
In development
website:
www.m2epower.com

SolarRolls

Though the company primarily makes traditional navigational devices and camping supplies, Brunton also produces a rugged, powerful line of portable solar panels available in three sizes and energy grades for off-the-grid use. SolarRolls, the company's first flexible panels, combine the portability of compact photovoltaics with the surface area normally used by large residential and commercial panels.

With maximum outputs of 4.5 to 14 watts depending on the model, SolarRolls set the standard for consumer photovoltaics. Intense product development yielded a waterproof, flexible, amorphous solar cell that performs well even in low light. Constructed out of Tefzel fluoropolymer, the cell is also extremely durable. Each unit comes equipped with multilinking cables, allowing the user to connect multiple SolarRolls for increased energy output. The rolls can power satellite phones, gadgets, cameras, Brunton's peripheral car battery, and even low-energy laptop computers. The three models—SolarRoll 4.5, SolarRoll 9, and SolarRoll 14—are each 12 inches (30 cm) wide and range from 22 to 57 inches (56 to 145 cm) in length. Durable and compactly efficient, SolarRolls are applicable in rural, developing world, and outdoor contexts.

designer:
    Brunton
geographical implementation/
market/availability:
    Global, via website
status:
    Consumer product
price:
    $295 and up
website:
    www.brunton.com

Solio Classic Universal Hybrid Charger

designer:
Better Energy Systems, Ltd.
**geographical implementation/
market/availability:**
Global, via website
status:
Consumer product
price:
$99.95
website:
www.solio.com

The Solio Classic Universal Hybrid Charger is compact enough to carry anywhere and powerful enough to charge all handheld electronics using renewable solar energy. Just one hour of sunshine for the Solio equals 20 minutes of talking on a cell phone or 50 minutes of listening to an mp3 player for a user. To maximize photovoltaic surface area, three panels, resembling a flower's petals, fold out of the pod-shaped charger. Able to harvest energy from the sun or a wall plug, the Solio's hybrid nature makes it applicable in emergency and off-the-grid situations. The device charges at the same rate as traditional travel adapters and comes with a variety of connections to accommodate almost all gadgets.

Solio is produced by Better Energy Systems, a UK-based company that develops and markets portable clean-technology products for travel, work, and play. The firm's offerings are comfortable steps toward sustainability for consumers, allowing users to commit to more environmentally friendly and energy-independent lifestyles with virtually no inconvenience.

Sugarcane Charcoal

In Haiti, the poorest country in the Western Hemisphere, the primary cooking fuel is wood charcoal. The fuel is notoriously dirty when burned, and many children in the country die of respiratory infections due to inhalation of indoor cooking fumes. Despite the charcoal's detriments, Haitians are dependent on it, which is additionally problematic because Haiti is 98 percent deforested. As a potential solution to these issues, a team of engineers and students, led by Amy Smith from MIT's D-Lab, looked to agricultural waste as a viable resource for the production of cleaner, more sustainable charcoal that could simultaneously create jobs and fuel.

The charcoal the team developed is made from dried bagasse, the primary waste product from sugarcane processing. This fibrous material is left after the juice has been squeezed from the cane. The bagasse is burned in a 55-gallon (208-L) oil-drum kiln, where it carbonizes. It is then mixed with cassava root as a binder and compacted using a press designed by D-Lab to form briquettes. The charcoal burns clean, creating no smoke and making it healthier to use and produce. As it requires no wood, it also preserves the little forest Haiti has left. Though the sugarcane has been successful, D-Lab continues to research and explore other agricultural waste products, such as corncobs, that could be cooking-fuel alternatives. In its new use, sugarcane charcoal gives waste products a function and creates jobs to support its continued production, while using local materials and skills to support new enterprises and sustain emerging economies. Since its initial implementation in Haiti, the use and production of sugarcane charcoal has been field-tested and expanded into parts of Brazil, Ghana, and India, places where sugarcane and its agricultural waste are widely available.

energy
+ food, enterprise

designer:
D-Lab at the Massachusetts
Institute of Technology (MIT)
other partners/clients/producers:
Friends of Petite Anse
**geographical implementation/
market/availability:**
Brazil, Ghana, Haiti, India;
on project basis
status:
Project implemented
website:
web.mit.edu/d-lab

Weza Portable Energy Source

Freeplay Energy is known for making durable and affordable devices that are powered by clean energies including solar, hand-crank, and—in the case of the Weza—"step" power. The versatile product is tough yet portable and delivers dependable power in emergency or off-the-grid situations. The Weza transforms human steps into power using its built-in foot treadle. The treadle operates similarly to a pump: The user steps on it repeatedly to generate energy. Its internal rechargeable 12-volt battery can jump-start cars or other engines and devices, creating electrical energy of 25 to 40 watts depending on the effort applied.

The Weza can also be charged via AC, DC, wind, or solar power; it is completely energy independent, with no need for a power grid or batteries. Its foldable arms make it easy to carry and store, while its included jumper cables and tool kit make it a full-service, mobile power station ideal to be kept in cars, motor homes, boats, or rural houses. Because of its robust capacity and energy independence, the Weza can also provide consistent power to communities in the developing world. It is constructed from high-quality electrical and mechanical materials and components. Its rugged, dependable design is representative of all of Freeplay's product offerings, which make the case for accessible energy on a global scale. The word weza means "power" or "to be empowered" in Swahili.

designer:
    Freeplay Energy
geographical implementation/ market/availability:
    Global, via website and dealers
status:
    Consumer product
price:
    $299.99
website:
    www.freeplayenergy.com

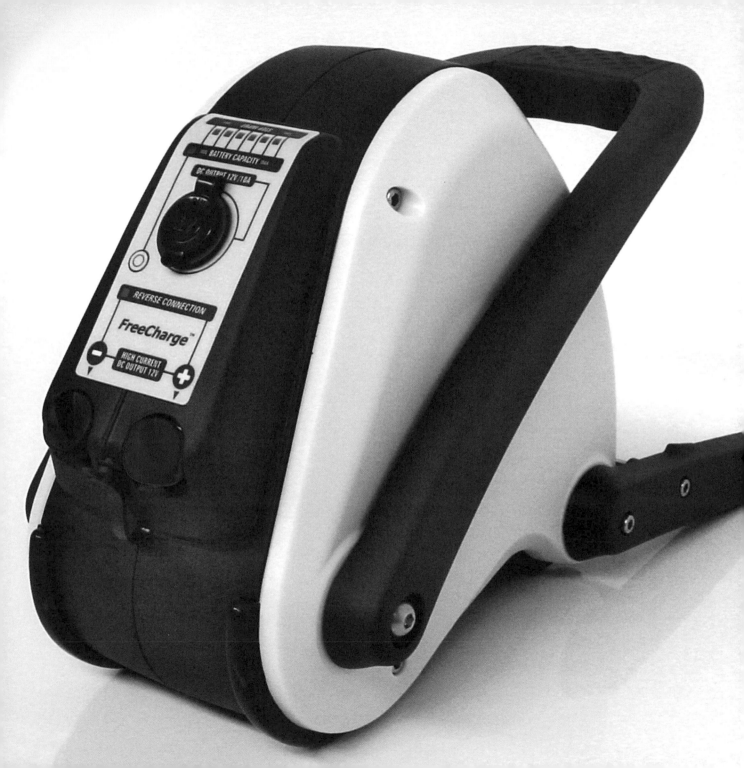

Windbelt

designer:
Humdinger Wind Energy, LLC
geographical implementation/ market/availability:
Global
status:
In development
website:
www.humdingerwind.com

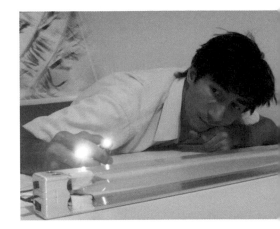

Unlike most wind-based technologies that rely on turbines entirely, the Windbelt eschews them altogether. While working in Haiti, Shawn Frayne, president of Humdinger Wind Energy, recognized the need for scalable wind power for household devices. However, he knew that the conventional turbine, the only commercially viable wind-energy device available at the time, was not suitable for such uses. Through Frayne's innovation and research, Humdinger has developed Windbelt, an integrated energy technology that relies on an aerodynamic phenomenon called aeroelastic flutter. This is the same phenomenon that caused the Tacoma Narrows Bridge to fall in 1940, but Humdinger has used this usually destructive force to produce energy on a variety of scales.

Once developed, Windbelt would be integrated into other devices or systems, rather than acting as a freestanding energy generator. It is made of a taut membrane outfitted with two magnets that oscillate between metal coils and essentially pull energy from the wind. This action is similar to a blade of grass that vibrates between your fingers and makes a whistling sound. As the wind vibrates the coils, that energy is harnessed. The energy of the moving membrane is then translated to usable electricity through newly developed linear generators. In short, the Windbelt uses the wind's ability to move a long, taut object, rather than to rotate a turbine. Tests have shown that in low-speed winds Windbelt is 10 to 30 times more efficient than the best microturbines. The technology is also made from inexpensive parts and is easy to repair, making it applicable for the developing world and emerging markets.

The product's clean technology has been used on a range of scales, from micro (data sensors) to medium (lighting, cell phones, and wireless routers) to large (infrastructural communication networks). Windbelt promotes both energy efficiency and cheaper, more ubiquitous energy generation through a renewable resource. Humdinger is a research and development firm committed to quickly disseminating the Windbelt technology to a variety of markets through licensing or assignment of the technology to industry partners.

education

Round the number 124 to the nearest hundred.

Educational Applications for the Apple iPhone

designers:
Various
other partners/clients/producers:
Apple
geographical implementation/ market/availability:
Global, via website
status:
Consumer product
price:
Up to $40
website:
www.apple.com/iphone/appstore

When introduced in 2008, Apple's 3G iPhone provided increased technological abilities as compared to both its earlier model and other cell phones. These advancements included the integration of applications (apps) for interests ranging from social networking to stock market monitoring to knowledge-based learning. The educational apps—which are developed by third-party companies, sold through Apple's iTunes software, and downloaded directly to an iPhone—deliver learning interfaces through the convenience of the mobile phone. Many believe that the cell phone, not the laptop, is the device that has the potential to connect and educate billions worldwide, and the addition of educational software to a phone's service offerings strengthens that case.

For children and adults alike, the iPhone's suite of educational apps offers learning experiences in literacy, languages, science, vocabulary, math, geography, logic, reasoning, and more. Some apps function like flash cards, others like e-books, and others rely on game interfaces to improve learning through brain-building exercises. For example, Lexicon's apps help users learn more than 70 languages using animated flash cards and quizzes. Users can also create and play back audio recordings to measure progress. Starmap is a "pocket planetarium" that teaches the basics of constellations, planets, stargazing techniques, and other astronomy topics, while Modality has produced Kindergarten to 12th-grade curricular learning apps and flash cards for neuroscience and geography.

By combining elementary and advanced educational tools with the portability and convenience of the cell phone, Apple's offerings use an existing infrastructure to allow for personalized learning experiences.

Enabling Devices

designer:
Enabling Devices
**geographical implementation/
market/availability:**
Global, via website or catalogue
status:
Consumer product
price:
$10–$500
website:
www.enablingdevices.com

Enabling Devices, a company founded by Steven E. Kanor, PhD, is committed to the development and distribution of educational and assistive toys and tools for those with disabling conditions. The devices are designed specifically for the needs of those with autism, Down syndrome, cerebral palsy, and other emotional and physical impairments to encourage communication, play, and development of motor skills. Both children and adults benefit from use of the company's products.

Devices include electromechanical systems such as capability switches and communicators. The switches allow users to activate reactions, such as lights and sounds, helping those with autism or other physically challenging conditions understand cause-and-effect connections by relating their actions to changes in their physical environments. The design of the devices takes into consideration factors including the body parts and senses the user has control over, the user's limitations in range of motion,

and the user's need to be motivated to take action. To accommodate these and other issues, the product line includes hand, finger, and body switches; light, vibration, and music switches; sip, puff, and breath switches; and textured and pillow switches. When a user engages the switch or communicator, reactions ranging from sound, light, or other tactile responses are cued. Many devices are wirelessly connected to distant receivers, while others are optimized for wheelchair users. By relating the activation of a switch to an immediate effect (the appearance of light, music, or other effect), the user is able to better connect his own actions to consequent results as a means of understanding his surroundings.

Similarly, communicators are assistive technology devices for use in the classroom or home. They serve as creative learning and teaching tools to encourage expressive language and enable the building of cognitive skills. These devices give people who are nonverbal or speech impaired a

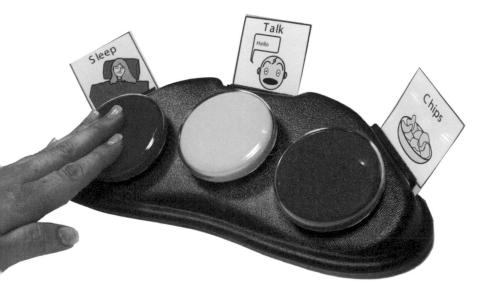

voice, through buttons that trigger prerecorded words and phrases, and through nonaural tools. The Go! Board communicator, for example, is designed specifically for early development in special-education classrooms. Picture and symbol tiles that signify chores and activities can be arranged to visually outline a schedule for the student. When a task is completed, the tile can be removed from the board and replaced with another. On the Phrase Maker Communicator, cards bearing a word and image are paired with buttons. When the student hits a button, the recorded voice says the word, allowing the user to connect visual cues to construct full sentences.

Enabling Devices has long been known for the innovation of its in-house design teams. Their product offerings enable people with physical and behavioral challenges to communicate, learn, work, and play. Whether inside or outside a classroom, the devices give users the ability to live more easily, efficiently, and enjoyably.

Kinkajou Microfilm Projector and Portable Library

designer:
Design that Matters
other partners/clients/producers:
US Agency for International Development (USAID), World Education, project volunteers from Babson, Cambridge, Harvard, and other colleges and universities, professional volunteers from Fisher-Price, Optikos, and ChipWrights
geographical implementation/ market/availability:
Global, on project basis
status:
Limited distribution
price:
Approx. $15
website:
www.designthatmatters.org

Addressing inconsistent access to both quality education and electricity in the developing world, the Kinkajou Microfilm Projector and Portable Library brings nighttime literacy instruction to underserved demographics. The initiative for Kinkajou's development began in 2002 and has been spearheaded by Boston-based nonprofit Design that Matters. With increased literacy, communities and individual citizens in the developing world are empowered to start businesses, attend vocational training programs, or, more basically, successfully read prescription bottle labels and newspapers. However, since most adults in these areas work during the day and few communities have reliable access to electricity, there is little opportunity for many people to learn to read. Kinkajou addresses these challenges by combining a literacy library with a solar-powered projector for group learning after the sun has set.

The system is rugged, lightweight, and requires little energy. It stores up to 10,000 images, which are used to teach written words and phrases on a microfilm cassette at a fraction of the cost of traditional textbooks. The projector's light source is a 5-watt, white LED, rated to last 100,000 hours, which is approximately 11 years of operating time. Its 12-volt power pack and 12-watt solar panel allow the system to harvest a charge during the day for evening use.

In 2004, with funding from USAID, World Education implemented Kinkajou systems in literacy centers in 45 Malian villages. After two years of use, more than 3,000 adults in those areas had learned to read using the projectors. Teachers report that the learning method is more effective than traditional classroom instruction. Karamogo Moulaye Yatara, a literacy teacher from Ngoye, Mali, explains, "[The Kinkajou] is wonderful. The teacher doesn't spend time and energy searching images, or walking between tables to show them. We gain a lot of time."

Kinkajou transforms the way in which adult education is provided on a large scale. Projected texts serve as a standardized, higher-quality replacement for instructors' poor handwriting, and they expand deliverable content to full reference libraries rather than individual textbooks. Testing for potential integration of the projectors has taken place in Malian elementary schools, as well as in Bangladesh by Ashoka Fellow Muhammad Ibrahim and partners from the Center for Mass Education in Science.

Learning Landscape

Created by Project H Design fellows Heleen de Goey, Ilona de Jongh, Kristina Drury, Dan Grossman, and Neha Thatte, Learning Landscape is a scalable, grid-based playground system for elementary math education. Southern Uganda's Kutamba AIDS Orphans School, built by Matthew Miller in partnership with Architecture for Humanity, served as the case study and initial pilot installation of the outdoor classroom and playground. Because math is universal, Learning Landscape can be adapted for use in any country and can be tailored to a range of skill levels.

The designers conceived of 10 math-based games to be played within a square grid, which can be built in a four-by-four, five-by-five, or six-by-six configuration based on the number of students and the space constraints. For the Kutamba installation, a 16-point grid, measuring 25 by 25 feet (7.6 by 7.6 m), was constructed using reclaimed tires arranged inside a large sandbox.

The tires mark points on the grid, and during game play, numbers can be written directly on them with chalk. (The tires can also be used as outdoor classroom space when coupled with an integrated bench system.)

The 10 games teach concepts including addition, subtraction, multiplication, and division, as well as spatial and logical reasoning through individual and team-based competition. In Match Me, for example, students form two teams, and the teacher calls out a math question. Two students, one from each team, directly compete to solve the equation, locate the tire marked with the number that corresponds to the answer, and sit on top of it. The team member who finds the correct tire first returns to his team's line. The team whose players remain in line the longest wins.

Learning Landscape, though realized as a playground in its pilot installation, can be used on a variety of scales. Project H has continued its adaptation of the system, developing a product-sized version for in-classroom tabletop use based on the same grid games. Rather than focusing on a specific set of objects, the design's systems approach makes it an educational tool that is both universally adaptable and context specific.

designer:
    Project H Design
other partners/clients/producers:
    Matthew Miller, Kutamba AIDS Orphans School, Architecture for Humanity
geographical implementation/ market/availability:
    Global, on project basis
status:
    Limited distribution
website:
    www.projecthdesign.com

Max Chair

designer:
Tom Wates

other partners/clients/producers:
Don't Lean Back, Ltd. (DLB)

**geographical implementation/
market/availability:**
Global, via website and dealers

status:
Consumer product

price:
Approx. $25

website:
www.dlbltd.co.uk

Instead of yelling at unruly students who were leaning back in their chairs during class, Tom Wates, a physical education and math teacher in London, went to the drawing board to find a way to change the chairs themselves. The result is the Max Chair, a seat that cannot be tilted onto its back legs. After the design of the chair was complete, Wates and his investors formed DLB, a UK-based company that produces the chairs and other school furniture designed for student safety. The affordable classroom chair, which is available in four sizes to accommodate all ages, is made from polypropylene and steel and comes in six colors, including a black version that is made from recycled materials. The frame is ergonomically optimized for both comfort and safety. Without sacrificing a clean aesthetic, the angles and curvature of the chair's legs make tilting and leaning back close to impossible. The seat back also promotes proper posture, and all edges are smooth and child friendly. With 7,000 chair-related accidents occurring in UK schools every year, the product is a graceful solution to a real problem.

Mobee

designer:
Eddie Chiu
other partners/clients/
producers:
Parsons the New School for
Design, Helen Keller Services
for the Blind, United Cerebral
Palsy of New York City, Inc.
status:
Concept

For children with cerebral palsy and visual impairments, the ability to develop fine motor skills through movement and tactility is a key component in their young development. Mobee, a conceptual teaching tool developed by Parsons design student Eddie Chiu, is a training toy for such children who are two to five years old.

By playing with Mobee, children exercise the hand muscles crucial to motor development as they slide a knob though a concave path in connected blocks. The simple action, enhanced by color differentiation, increases hand-eye coordination and the ability to grasp and direct. As the knob slides through the groove, Mobee produces different sounds based on the texture of the path at different points. The textures may include raised dots, ribbings, or larger "speed bumps." The corresponding sounds engage aural sensations to further enhance the motion and feeling as users move along the course. Magnets are embedded within the sides of each block to allow for easy arrangement, rearrangement, disassembly, and varied configurations that continually change the learning experience. Additionally, blocks feature dry-erase surfaces, allowing parents and children to draw and create personalized narratives.

Montessori Toys

The Montessori method of elementary education encourages individual expression and learning through creativity and play by providing a flexible educational platform for natural development and wholesome growth. Through individual work and creation, children develop concentration and self-discipline at their own speeds within a supervised framework.

Developed in 1929 by Italian physician and child-development specialist Maria Montessori, the Montessori learning system differs from the traditional model. Instead of being asked only to absorb information, each child is put in charge of her own environment, guided by a teacher who helps her make good choices and carry out her own research, exploration, and creation.

Within this structure, it is the teacher's responsibility to provide thoughtful and inspiring materials and objects for the students' use and adaptation in the space. The classroom environment is traditionally organized according to subject area, while objects and toys follow international Montessori standards. The design of the materials began when Montessori observed that young children were intensely attracted to sensory development objects, and that they used them spontaneously, independently, and repeatedly with great concentration. She also saw that using the objects gave the children an immediate sense of accomplishment and encouragement.

Traditionally, Montessori toys are beautiful, symbolic, flexible, and simple in material and color to encourage personal engagement, understanding, and application by each student. Literacy toys, for example, consist of simple, three-dimensional, colored shapes, each representing a grammatical structure, part of speech, or punctuation symbol. Mathematical relationships are learned using red and blue rods of different lengths that demonstrate measurement and quantitative relationships, and fraction skittles, which are small figures divided into two, three, or four pieces

designer:
    Maria Montessori
other partners/clients/producers:
    Individual manufacturers and
    distributors
**geographical implementation/
market/availability:**
    Global, via websites and dealers
status:
    Consumer product
price:
    $10–$150

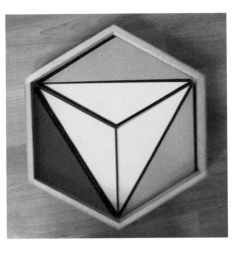

to represent fractional comparisons. Arithmetic and algebraic cubes integrate pieces of different colors and sizes to visually and kinesthetically teach additive concepts.

Montessori materials are unique in their simple elements, which require an individual creativity to bring meaning to their use and construction. Because the toys are also comprised of many individual parts, they may be used together through building and combining, further encouraging learning by making students engage with a tangible material. "The Montessori method is based on the spontaneous activity of the child, which is aroused precisely by the interest the child takes in the material," Montessori explained.

Though not a designer herself, Montessori saw the value in the aesthetics of the toys used in her method, viewing their beauty as an invitation to play and learn. "All the apparatus must be meticulously in order, beautiful and shiny, in perfect condition," she instructed. "Nothing must be missing, so that to the child it always seems new, complete, and ready for use."

Oblo

designer:
  Marko Pavlovic
**geographical implementation/
market/availability:**
  Global
status:
  In development
website:
  www.marko-pavlovic.com

Numerous educational theories recognize tactile play as a powerful learning tool. Through its design, Oblo, a spherical didactic puzzle, manifests those theories and blurs the line between play and learning. The ball has a sphere at its core and is made up of three concentric layers or shells, each of which is comprised of multiple pieces. Each of the 10 total pieces is a different size and shape, its color corresponding to its layer. The shells must be twisted against the sphere's central axis in order to successfully remove individual pieces from the center of the ball, until all pieces have been removed and the Oblo has been entirely disassembled. The ball may then be reassembled in a similar fashion.

Though the task it presents is a seemingly simple one, Oblo can be modified for different age groups and skill levels by enlarging or shrinking the open space in the outer layer or using a larger variety of shapes. The diameter of the outer layer shell can also be expanded, increasing the thickness of each internal layer.

For all ages the object teaches spatial geometry and fine motor skills, exercising and training the three muscle groups necessary for hand-eye coordination: fingers and hand for grasping, index finger and thumb for pinching, and wrist for rotation. Oblo was designed by a first-year student from the School of Design at the University of Zagreb and was honored with a 2008 IDEA Award from the Industrial Designers Society of America. The toy is an example of a didactic product that engages color and shape elements for both children and adults, bridging markets through design.

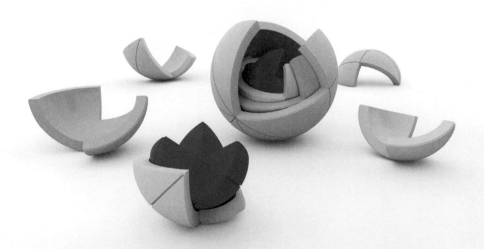

One Laptop Per Child: XO and XOXO Laptops

page 173
Design Revolution
education

The highly publicized XO Laptop, designed by Yves Behar–led fuseproject for the nonprofit One Laptop Per Child (OLPC), is an example of a collaborative, high-quality design and technology solution for the developing world. It has been both lauded for its innovation and social impact and critiqued for its imperfections and promotion of "leapfrogging" technologies in the developing world. The new XOXO laptop has been redesigned based on the strengths and failures of the original. The product's evolution is an outstanding case study in design entrepreneurship—and perhaps the limits of what "good design" can deliver.

The original XO laptop, intended to cost just $100 per unit, was designed to be a revolutionary device that would bring information, networking, and communication to children in underserved demographics, who in many cases had never touched a computer, much less had one of their own. The laptop was a feat of energy efficiency and engineering, running on 10 percent of the energy traditional laptops required and integrating clean-energy chargers like hand cranks, solar-panel or wind-turbine peripherals, and a yo-yo–style kinetic charger. Its design was both anthropomorphic and iconic, its capabilities robust yet expressive, challenging what a laptop could do and be. With more than 10 contributing partners, the development of XO was truly a collaboration, which some have argued was to the product's detriment.

More than 600,000 XOs are currently in use worldwide. They are primarily distributed through government purchases for schools, though OLPC ran a successful "buy one, give one" campaign during the 2007 holiday season, which was relaunched through Amazon.com in 2008. Its consumer availability proves the point of some detractors who argue that the product may be better suited for consumer markets than developing countries, where the leap to using such an innovative machine has been unsuccessful in academic environments.

designers:
> fuseproject, One Laptop Per Child (OLPC), Massachusetts Institute of Technology (MIT) Media Lab

other partners/clients/producers:
> Advanced Micro Devices, Brightstar, Design Continuum, Inc., Freeplay Energy, Google, Intel Corp., Pentagram, Quanta Computer, Red Hat, SQUID Labs

geographical implementation/ market/availability:
> Global, via Amazon.com or on project basis through OLPC

status:
> Consumer product

price:
> $399 for Give One, Get One program

website:
> www.laptop.org

After the first-generation XO proved to be both a technological achievement and an opportunity for improvement, OLPC released the concept for the XOXO second-generation, folding tablet laptop in May 2008. The XOXO is half the size of the XO and features two touch screens. The new version expands on the XO's primary goal to bring collaborative learning platforms and networked computer access to children worldwide. The computer departs from a traditional keyboard and screen layout, and has new interfaces for "playing with" data and information to increase understanding. The smaller, more compact format also addresses the issue of cost, since the $100 target was never met for the XO. "Based on feedback from governments, educators, and most important, the children themselves, we are aggressively working to lower the cost, power, and size of the XO laptop so that it is more affordable and usable by the world's poorest children," states Nicholas Negroponte, founder and chairman of OLPC. XOXO, once in distribution, will use lower-consumption power systems, leave a smaller footprint, and feature an enhanced, booklike learning experience. The XOXO is set to become widely available in early 2010.

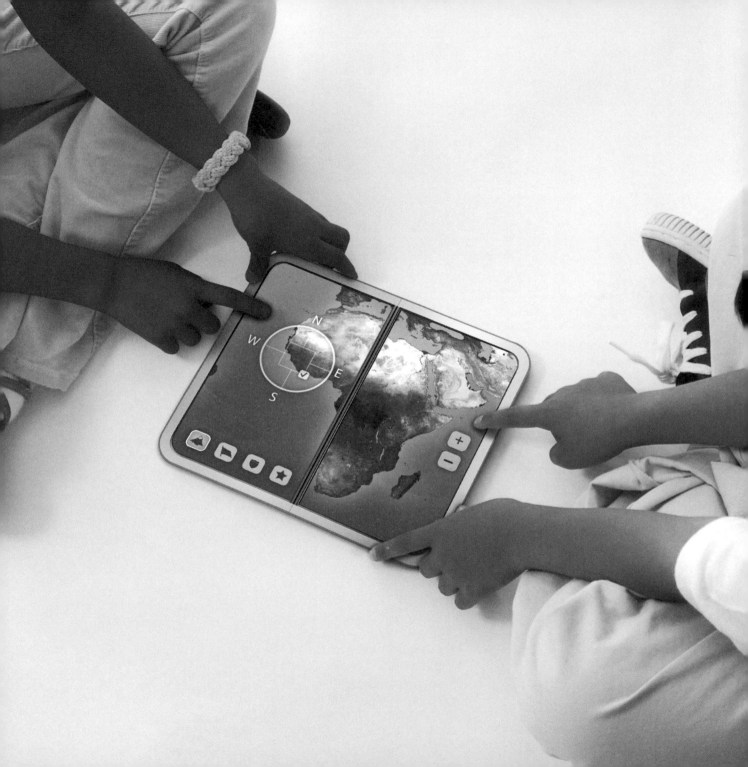

Ordrup School

designer:
  Bosch & Fjord
other partners/clients/producers:
  SKUB (Danish school
  development and expansion
  project)
**geographical implementation/
market/availability:**
  Gentofte, Denmark
status:
  Project implemented
website:
  www.bosch-fjord.com

In designing the Ordrup School for six- to 12-year-old students in Gentofte, Denmark, Danish firm Bosch & Fjord prioritized the creation of differentiated spaces for teaching and creative thinking for children. Though the school represents innovative leaps in educational space planning, it is the objects within the classrooms that create engaging learning environments for children. The design elements are based around three concepts: peace and absorption, discussion and cooperation, and security and presence. Through the separation of these themes and their corresponding objects in the space, the designers created contrasts that isolate activities for optimal and concentrated learning.

Raised window seating provides students with views of the outside world, and green platforms with red Hot Pots—seating areas that multiple students can step down into—function as spaces for individual quiet reading or physical play. In the classrooms for younger students, where peace and absorption are the priority, tubes in which children can sit and read provide security and solace, while movable pieces of carpet become flexible, personal spaces for work and play. In the classrooms for midlevel grades, Hot Pots create forum spaces for small groups, and concentration booths provide areas for individual respite and focus. In the rooms for the oldest students, which prioritize personal expression, bright red sofas and long tables foster social interactions and a flexible framework for learning. Through a close collaboration with students and teachers, Bosch & Fjord brought to life a school in which every object and space is both functional and didactic.

Spark

designer:
    IDEO
other partners/clients/producers:
    Project Inkwell
**geographical implementation/
market/availability:**
    Global
status:
    Concept
website:
    www.projectinkwell.com

To bring innovative educational technologies into Kindergarten to 12th-grade classrooms, Project Inkwell, a company that creates standards for the integration of technology into schools worldwide, partnered with IDEO to design Spark, a concept for a mobile learning tool. The device aims to inspire students to learn anywhere and everywhere, combining wireless capabilities with multimedia interfaces that promote education and exploration on an individual basis and in the classroom.

After conducting extensive fieldwork with educational and technology experts, students, and teachers to determine children's needs, Project Inkwell and IDEO developed Spark to encourage interaction between all parties in the educational system and promote the sharing and publishing of knowledge to make it collectively available. Spark has a soft, brightly colored case and a replaceable keyboard and spare battery that ensure easy maintenance. Its interface accommodates individual learning

experiences as well as networked learning for both teacher-to-student and student-to-student communication. Through the development of the product and other learning devices, Project Inkwell is continuing its mission to set standards for educational infrastructures and to ensure that innovative, appropriate technologies reach young students around the world.

Tack-Tiles Braille System

Around the world, literacy is generally accepted as a foundation for academic studies; however, only about 10 percent of visually impaired children have access to quality literacy education. Designed and produced by Kevin Murphy, who holds a doctorate in parenting and disability studies and whose son is blind, Tack-Tiles are Braille-based blocks that teach basic and advanced reading and comprehension. Since 1994 they have been used to aid students on every level, from elementary schools to PhD programs, serving as valuable tactile aids when vision is not the primary means of learning.

The Tack-Tiles Braille System, which is based on the stackable properties of LEGO blocks, is a highly applicable and sophisticated teaching tool for various academic subjects. The system is available in English, French, German, Italian, and Spanish, as well as Nemeth Braille Code for Mathematics, Braille for music notation, and computer Braille code. Used as a tool for teachers

of both blind and visually impaired children, the tiles have printed and raised Braille code on their surfaces for tactile, interactive, and progressive learning. Each of the blocks represents a letter, number, syllable, punctuation mark, or word and is used in combination with other blocks. They are placed atop a special board to create words, sentences, games, equations, musical compositions, and more. Murphy stresses that there is no right way to use Tack-Tiles, but rather that they serve as a platform for personalized learning. In some of its most advanced applications, the system has been used in college-level chemistry and math courses to teach complex concepts. For Murphy those uses stand out as significant achievements of his invention. "There was a freshman at a college in Illinois who used Tack-Tiles to master quadratic equations . . . . He spent two months stuck in the mud before help came," he recalls. Product accessories such as the Tack-Tiles Braille TEASER puzzle and the Tack-Tiles (Computer) KEYPAD

for IntelliKeys have been added to the company's offerings to expand the reach of the tools across disciplines and technologies.

designer:
Kevin Murphy
geographical implementation/ market/availability:
Global, via website
status:
Consumer product
price:
$695
website:
www.tack-tiles.com

Treeblocks Math Kit

designer:
Treeblocks
other partners/clients/producers:
HighReach Learning
**geographical implementation/
market/availability:**
Global, via website
status:
Consumer product
price:
$64.95
website:
www.treeblocks.com

The Math Kit from Treeblocks includes a set of 66 precisely measured wood pieces designed to teach relational math principles to children and adults. The set's blocks, which range in length from .4 to 4.7 inches (1 to 12 cm), teach spatial reasoning, problem solving, proportions, and motor skills. The kit includes a 96-card activity deck that suggests physical and visual math exercises on three difficulty levels for use with the blocks.

Treeblocks can be used as normal play blocks or stacked to perform mathematical equations, a technique historically used by the Greeks and Egyptians as a means of measurement. For example, to represent a simple addition equation, the user would place a number of the smaller pieces in a vertical line adjacent to one of the larger pieces, visually discovering what combination of smaller numbers must be added together to equal a larger one. Pieces are made from discarded wood from managed paper forests or from abandoned or end-of-cycle apple, cherry, or hazelnut trees purchased directly from farmers.

Voting Ruler

designer:
concentrate design, ltd.
geographical implementation/market/availability:
Global, via website
status:
Consumer product
price:
$5
website:
www.concentrate.org.uk

Teachers' ability to measure their students' comprehension is as integral to the classroom educational process as the instruction itself. If teachers can better assess how many students understand particular lessons and which individuals are struggling with certain concepts, they can better tailor their instruction to focus on specific ideas and work with students who may need extra help.

The Voting Ruler is a simple tool that works as a traditional ruler for measuring, as well as a yes-or-no diagnostic for students to signal whether or not they understand a topic taught in class. In response to a teacher's question, a student simply raises his ruler with either the end marked "yes" or the end marked "no" in the air. The teacher can then immediately gauge the understanding of individuals and the larger group. Because the ruler's icons are color coded, small, and forward facing, which takes

them out of the view of other pupils, students need not be embarrassed to answer "no" to the question. Using a tool rather than raising a hand also engages children and encourages involvement in lessons.

UK-based concentrate design is dedicated to the exploration of how design can enhance educational experiences for young children, parents, and students.

mobility

A2B Light Electric Vehicle

Given that many urban commuters travel only a few miles each day, the market for short-range, high-performance personal transportation is undeniable. The A2B Light Electric Vehicle has "the heart of a bicycle and the soul of a scooter." When its electric motor is in use, the bike has a range of 20 miles (33 km) and a maximum speed of 20 miles per hour (33 km/h), which is more than sufficient for most daily trips to and from work, the market, or other local destinations. An optional secondary lithium-ion battery can double the distance capability, or the A2B can be pedaled like a traditional, nonelectric bicycle. Simply plug the bike in to recharge or manually pedal when it has no battery power.

The compact electric bike boasts full suspension, an oversized, comfortable seat, and a touch-pedal system. Its frame is constructed from lightweight aluminum, making it easy to transport or carry, and it can accommodate up to two bags and two baskets for cargo. The A2B provides a healthy, environmentally friendly transportation option that is versatile, reliable, and economical for urban and suburban use. Ultra Motor has a full line of light electric vehicles and is committed to helping consumers integrate the transportation mode into their daily routines for affordability, sustainability, fitness, and fun.

mobility
+ well-being, play

designer:
Ultra Motor
**geographical implementation/
market/availability:**
USA, Canada; via dealers
status:
Consumer product
price:
$2,599
website:
www.ultramotor.com

designer:
Institute for Affordable
Transportation (IAT)
other partners/clients/producers:
VBM de Honduras
**geographical implementation/
market/availability:**
Global, via IAT
status:
Limited distribution
price:
Up to $3,300
website:
www.drivebuv.org

Basic Utility Vehicle (BUV)

For merchants and farmers in the developing world, access to affordable, reliable transportation can boost profits and product capacities and significantly increase quality of life. The Basic Utility Vehicle is, as the name implies, a utilitarian vehicle for transporting people and cargo. In many regions the BUV can compensate for a lack of infrastructure by providing a connection between two often-visited points. The vehicles are commonly used as school buses, ambulances, construction equipment vehicles, and farm transportation.

Designed by IAT in collaboration with hundreds of student and professional engineers, the BUV costs $3,300 when manufactured in the USA and less when built locally in developing countries. Its frame can accommodate loads of up to 1,200 pounds (544 kg), while extra power sources and a built-in grain grinder provide increased functionality.

BUVs can be produced locally in microfactories, which are given access to the design schematics and assistance in the training of workers and maintenance facilities by IAT. Through the BUV's local production and the mobility it enables, in areas where the vehicles are used profits increase, jobs are created, and individual enterprises become more robust and sustainable for household and community wealth. The product is easily built, repaired, and understood, making it an accessible, feasible option in a wide range of contexts.

The vehicles, which have also been distributed in parts of Africa, are currently most widely used in Honduras. Indianapolis-based IAT continues to research mobility issues in the developing world and runs its annual BUV competition to promote the vehicle and generate new ideas and applications for it.

Bikedispenser

Bringing the convenience of a vending machine to pedal-powered transportation, Bikedispenser is a Dutch system that makes renting a bike easy and affordable. In Arnhem and Nijmegen, the two cities in which the system has been implemented, the fully automated rental units, which each accommodate up to 100 bicycles, are located at train stations, transportation hubs, and parking garages, allowing for maximum accessibility and creating a seamless link to other forms of transportation. Commuters, companies, and local governments have all purchased memberships to the current systems. There are plans for the Bikedispenser system to expand to other cities in the coming years.

Thanks to Bikedispenser's corporate partnerships, membership in the program includes access to 100 other traditional bike rental locations throughout The Netherlands. Members of the program are given a card that, when held to the dispenser's reader, issues a bicycle in 15 seconds for just $3.75 for use up to 20 hours. When the renter is done with the bike, she returns it to the indicated depository and the transaction is complete. Bikedispenser offers a unique solution to the problems of how to both use and house shared bicycles. Its built-in storage unit ensures security and reliability.

designers:
Springtime, Post en Dekker
other partners/clients/producers:
OV-fiets, Gazelle, GreenChoice
**geographical implementation/
market/availability:**
The Netherlands, at rental
stations
status:
Limited distribution
price:
$3.75 per rental
website:
www.bikedispenser.com

Calfee Bamboo Bike

Craig Calfee began designing and building bicycles in 1987, after a bike collision left him wondering how to make a tougher bike frame. Since then his company, Calfee Design, has built some of the world's highest-quality custom bike frames for performance and durability, including one of its trademark designs, the Calfee Bamboo Bike. Begun as a publicity stunt in 1996, the bike, whose frame is made entirely of bamboo, evolved into a popular model that was officially added to the Calfee line in 2005.

More than just visually interesting, the bike provides better vibration damping than traditional carbon fiber bikes and has good structural stiffness, while the lightweight frame weighs just four to six pounds (1.8 to 2.7 kg). The bike is available in three frame shapes and can be customized to suit specific needs.

After its commercial launch, Calfee Design expanded production of the model into a developing market in an attempt to apply the same high-quality design to a more need-based area. On a trip across Africa in 1984, Craig Calfee had three observations that would inform the Bamboo Bikes in Africa initiative more than 20 years later: Bamboo was abundant, bikes were popular but undersupplied, and many people needed jobs. In 2007, thanks to a partnership with The Earth Institute at Columbia University, the initiative was launched to assist entrepreneurs in the developing world with making their own bicycles out of locally sourced bamboo. Beginning with an enterprise in Ghana, Calfee

designer:
Calfee Design
other partners/clients/producers:
The Earth Institute at Columbia University, Cyclists for Cultural Exchange
geographical implementation/ market/availability:
Global, via website
status:
Consumer product
price:
$2,700–$3,200
website:
www.calfeedesign.com

has helped to establish a sustainable business that caters to local needs. Durable mountain bikes and cargo bikes are available for purchase through the microbusiness. Given that bicycles are in great demand for transporting people and cargo in the country, the Calfee Bamboo Bike delivers a much-needed product, but also relies on local jobs, labor, and investment, creating a self-sufficient and scalable economic entity for community benefit and development. Calfee continues to work with the Ghanaian group and has plans to set

up additional microbusinesses for the production and local sales of the bike in additional locations in Ghana and across Africa.

designer:
Worldbike
**geographical implementation/
market/availability:**
Global, via website
status:
Project implemented
price:
Materials approx. $100
website:
www.worldbike.org

Chop 'N Drop Worldbike

Worldbike is an international network of designers, leaders, and development professionals in the bicycle industry working to provide efficient and affordable bike transportation and income-generating opportunities for the world's poor. Their motto is "Bikes that haul, for all." Rather than shipping bikes to locations in need, the organization creates and distributes bicycle designs that can be built locally.

Offering a simple solution to the problem of cargo transportation in the developing world, the group has created the Chop 'N Drop. The design for the bike is an open-source version of Worldbike's best-known product, the cargo-hauling Big Boda. The new version is durable and inexpensive to make for small production in the developing world. It also continues Worldbike's focus on outfitting bikes to carry heavy cargo for those for whom such transport is otherwise problematic. To construct the Chop 'N Drop, small-scale manufacturing facilities or skilled individuals cut a basic mountain-bike frame behind the seat tube, extending it to accommodate cargo racks or other carrying vessels. All users need a MIG, TIG, or comparable welder. Depending on the state of the bicycle that is being modified, components such as tires, brake pads, and pedals may also be required. The finished product can be used to transport passengers and cargo, including water and agricultural material.

The bike's most unique feature, however, is its open-source design. It allows the user to be builder and co-designer, or if the tools required are unavailable to individuals, the design can be implemented by local manufacturers, enabling grassroots enterprises to emerge.

JOURNEY Bi-Cruciate Stabilized Knee System

designer:
Herbst LaZar Bell

other partners/clients/producers:
Smith & Nephew

geographical implementation/ market/availability:
Global, to healthcare professionals

status:
Limited distribution

website:
www.journeyknee.com

Smith & Nephew, an innovator in the development of cutting-edge medical products and techniques, partnered with design firm Herbst LaZar Bell in the production of the JOURNEY Bi-Cruciate Stabilized Knee System. The artificial knee makes the case that "normal is extraordinary," providing knee-replacement patients with the ability to easily bend their legs, stand and sit for long periods of time, and perform other everyday movements.

Most knee replacements involve the conventional Total Knee Arthroplasty (TKA) technique, a procedure that does not restore normal knee kinematics. The resulting abnormal motions are primarily caused by changes to the structure of tissues like the anterior cruciate ligament (ACL). The JOURNEY Knee, a prosthetic for post-TKA patients, is expertly formed and highly engineered to support the normal leg stability, strength, flexion, and function that TKA often hinders. The knee is bi-cruciate stabilized, meaning it functions as a replacement for both the ACL and the posterior cruciate ligament (PCL). Both ligaments provide leg stability but are often removed during TKA procedures.

The development of the knee system grew from increased research and insight into surgeon and patient needs. Using newly developed tools for simulation and analysis, Smith & Nephew, along with Herbst LaZar Bell, looked closely at the kinetics and surfaces of a knee and translated specific features into a mechanical form that optimized performance and normalcy of motion. The system offers a wider range of sizing options and works with a specially designed set of instruments to facilitate increased precision during surgery, fitting, and adjustment. Made from Smith & Nephew's proprietary material, OXINIUM oxidized zirconium, the JOURNEY system also offers increased durability.

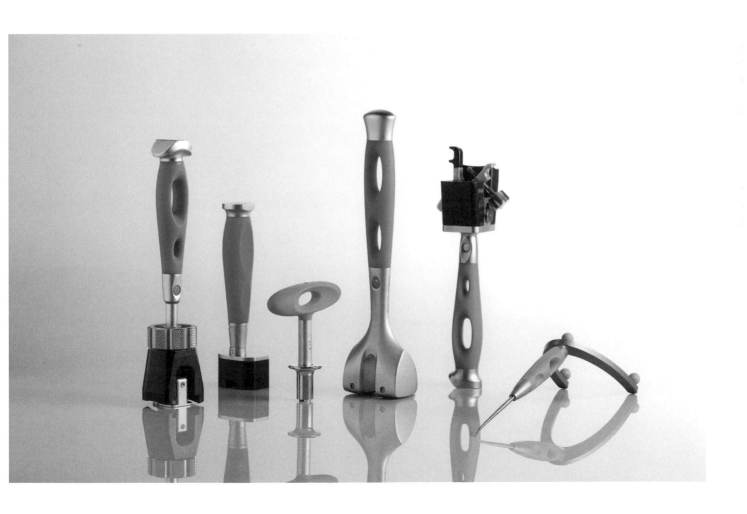

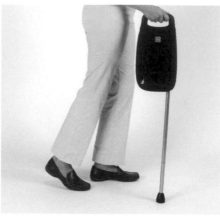

designer:
Michael Graves Design Group
other partners/clients/producers:
Drive Medical Design &
Manufacturing
**geographical implementation/
market/availability:**
Global, via Drive Medical
and dealers
status:
Limited distribution
website:
www.michaelgraves.com

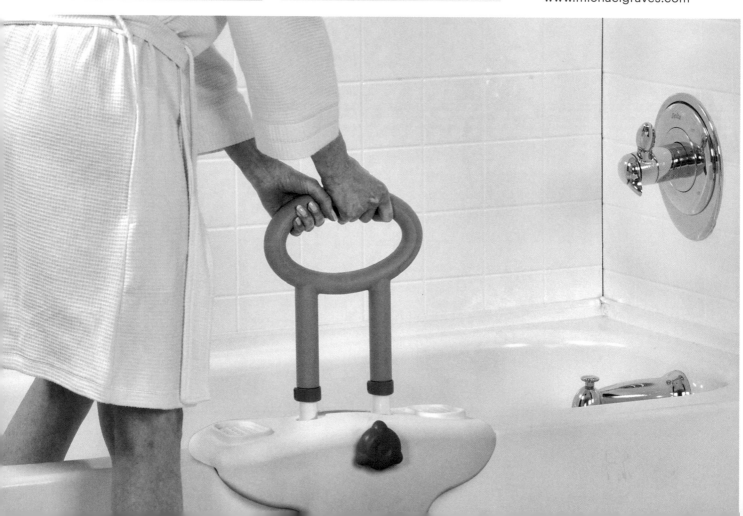

Michael Graves Collection for Drive Medical

In 2003 star architect and designer Michael Graves, whose portfolio includes everything from iconic buildings to household items sold at Target, was paralyzed from his midchest down after a virus destroyed nerves in his spinal cord. Instead of viewing the disability as debilitating, Graves saw in it a personal challenge and design opportunity. As he struggled with his own mobility and the objects that were supposedly designed to make his life easier, he embarked on a new mission: to create mobility tools for the disabled that actually ease day-to-day life. In an interview with journalist John Hockenberry, Graves explains, "People who become disabled have to radically redesign their outlook about the physical world. They redesign their sense of privacy and their sense of independence. Yet in the products they have to use, design has abandoned them."

To address the issue, Graves and his design team at Michael Graves Design Group began developing a line of durable medical equipment.

Its offerings, which are aesthetically appealing while catering to the user's medical needs, range from bath safety devices to walking aids, heating pads, and other tools for daily living. A collapsible walking stick, for example, caters directly to the user's desire for portability and style and folds into a built-in nylon case for easy storage in a bag or purse. Each of the designs focuses on ease of assembly, durability, and intuitive use. Details such as color cues (orange means adjustability, blue means personal care) create a brand language that unites the product line as a whole, while attention to ergonomics ensures the objects are focused on the user and his ease of motion. "We're changing the rules here, period," Graves states. "I want people to look at these objects and immediately get a message. The message I want is, 'Made by us, for us.'"

Through a partnership with medical equipment industry leader Drive Medical, Graves's products will be manufactured and mass-produced, bringing great solutions and dignity to a demographic underserved by the design community. The partnership, like Graves's alignment with other corporations such as Target and Disney, will use existing consumer venues to more widely distribute and promote the line. Drive Medical is known for its affordable, quality products and is one of the fastest-growing manufacturers of medical equipment in the healthcare industry.

Michael Graves Collection for Drive Medical may have emerged from personal frustration, but the development of the line represents something much greater: a shift in practice toward thinking about design for those who need it most. Now back at work full time, fueled by urgency and a worthy imperative, Graves says, "I have a new outlook on how improved design can add ease and dignity to life for all people who are concerned with safety in the home and coping with disabilities."

Rapid Deployable System (RDS)

Developed primarily for use by military and crisis-relief workers, the RDS provides "quick-up" structures for modular expansion that are durable, efficient, and easy to assemble and disassemble. The systems can also connect to existing shelters to add space for short-term needs. The RDS comes in a variety of sizes and is comprised of articulated parts such as arches, legs, leg sleeves, and a connecting hub. A separate floor and cover complete the shelter's construction.

The RDS is made from extreme rugged materials and has a weather-proofed surface, making it durable in the harshest environments and allowing it to be used as a long-term structure in the developing world. Its PVC-coated, high-tenacity fabric can sustain winds of up to 65 miles per hour (105 km/h) and 2 inches (5.1 cm) of rain per hour. The system also has passive ventilation systems and components that are interchangeable with other RDS units. The structures can be erected in just minutes for use as medical suites, operation centers, food service locations, and areas for first responders. The largest RDS shelter measures 695 square feet (64.5 sq. m) when assembled and collapses to a 3-by-3.5-by-6-foot (0.9-by-1.1-by-1.8-m) bundle.

designer:
  Hoberman Associates, Inc.
other partners/clients/producers:
  Johnson Outdoors's Eureka! Tents
geographical implementation/ market/availability:
  Global, via Johnson Outdoors and dealers
status:
  Consumer product
price:
  $12,000 and up
website:
  www.eurekatents.com

SkySails

SkySails are large-scale wind propulsions for cargo vessels. In effect, they transform cargo ships with effective loads of 8 to 32 tons (7.1 to 28.5 T) into sailboats, capturing the wind as energy to carry the ships across oceans. Depending on the wind and ship cargo, SkySails can reduce a ship's annual fuel costs by 10 to 35 percent, and up to 50 percent for some ships in consistent optimal wind conditions. Maritime shipping is entirely dependent on oil, so as oil prices rise, SkySails are an economically viable and environmentally responsible alternative.

While the principles behind them are similar, SkySails differ from conventional sailing systems in that the sail is connected to the ship via a long towing rope rather than fitted to a mast. SkySails consist of three major components: the towing kite and rope, the launch and recovery system, and a control unit for automatic operation. An optional weather routing system can also be added, providing companies with a wind-optimized guide to direct their ships to the most cost-effective routes. The towing kite, similar in shape to a paraglider, is double walled and made from high-strength, waterproof textiles, giving the kite aerodynamic properties much like those of an airplane wing. The kite and tear-proof synthetic rope effectively pull the ship in the direction toward which the wind is blowing. The launch and recovery system manages the deployment and lowering of the kite, while the steering system operates automatically to align the kite relative to wind direction and force, ship course, and speed.

By integrating SkySails, cargo ships become more profitable, safe, practical, and efficient. Most cargo ships can easily be retrofitted with SkySails without significant impact to the existing ship's structure or systems.

designer:
  SkySails GmbH & Co. KG
**geographical implementation/
market/availability:**
  Global, via SkySails and dealers
status:
  Limited distribution
website:
  www.skysails.info

designer:
  SylvanSport
geographical implementation/
market/availability:
  Global, via dealers
status:
  Consumer product
price:
  $7,995
website:
  www.sylvansport.com

SylvanSport GO

Unofficially dubbed the "Swiss Army Knife of campers," the SylvanSport GO is a lightweight yet rugged vehicle for spur-of-the-moment adventures. At just 800 pounds (363 kg), it can be towed by almost any car and can switch from a storage trailer to wheeled tent with a few clicks and flips. Tom Dempsey, founder of SylvanSport, outdoorsman, and designer, calls the GO "mobile adventure gear."

The camper was designed with comfort and versatility in mind—a counterargument to the standard large, clunky, and heavy RVs and SUVs. Made from aluminum tubes, polyethylene plastic fenders, and a waterproof cover, the GO exemplifies a rugged, gear-inspired aesthetic. Its sleek and compact form is optimized for minimum drag and maximum fuel efficiency and allows the vehicle to carry its own weight in cargo. The camper transforms easily into a tent with a sleeping area equivalent to one-and-a-half king-sized beds. With a spare tire, LED lights, and built-in racks for equipment, the compact trailer delivers easy and comfortable toting and living capabilities. With its multiple uses and durability, SylvanSport's GO encourages mobile living that is simple, endlessly functional, and fun.

Tactile Wand

To navigate their environments, blind individuals worldwide have long relied on the "white stick"—a simple, long wand with which they detect obstacles. The tool, however, is literally nothing more than a long stick. South Korean designer Jin Woo Han's Tactile Wand is a white stick for the twenty-first century, a pocket-sized, technology-enhanced gadget that delivers practical, life-improving assistance to the visually impaired. Han's design, though currently only a concept, would use a distance sensor and a series of pulses to alert the user to surrounding obstacles: the stronger the pulse, the nearer the object. While the sensor technology itself is not groundbreaking (distance sensors are commonly found in laser tape measures and similar devices), the innovation is in its application.

The Tactile Wand, if produced, would be rechargeable and compact, proving more portable than the traditional stick. The designer acknowledges the wand's potential drawbacks, including its dependence on a battery charge and, in replacing the white stick, its removal of a universal symbol of the blind. However, the wand's potential benefits for the day-to-day lives of the visually impaired make the product worthy of further exploration.

designer:
Jin Woo Han
status:
Concept

Walk
Score

designer:
>Front Seat

**geographical implementation/
market/availability:**
>Canada, UK, USA; via website

status:
>Project implemented

price:
>Free

website:
>www.walkscore.com

In the quest for an alternative to car transportation, walking is perhaps the best—and most underrated—option for local mobility. Walk Score, a free online tool, calculates the walkability of the surrounding neighborhood of a given address, helping people find places to live or visit where walking is a viable option for transportation. Simply enter an address to calculate a location's score (on a scale of one to 100). A score of 90 to 100, for example, is classified as "Walkers's Paradise," while a score of zero to 24 is "Car-Dependent (Driving Only)." The website's patent-pending algorithm also locates nearby stores, restaurants, schools, parks, and more, providing an immediate listing of a neighborhood's walkable venues. Points are awarded based on the distance to the closest amenities in each category.

While public transit websites often offer trip planners, Walk Score, developed by civic software company Front Seat, encourages walking both as a viable mode of local transportation and a form of exercise. Perhaps more important, it makes the case for walking as a means to invigorate, enjoy, and invest in our local communities and neighborhoods.

In addition to the online tool, Walk Score offers a real estate tile, an icon showing walkability that is easily integrated into online real estate listings, and the Walk Score widget, which can be added to other websites and blogs.

Whirlwind RoughRider

In the 1980s, paraplegic engineer and wheelchair designer Ralf Hotchkiss traveled the world, working with doctors and patients to design and build wheelchairs from locally available materials. He found that in many areas the need for the chairs was urgent and severe. In an effort to continue his work and bring reliable, affordable mobility to the handicapped in developing countries, Hotchkiss founded Whirlwind Wheelchair International with Peter Pfaelzer, an engineering professor at the Institute for Civic and Community Engagement at SFSU. The organization works to create and support enterprises for local wheelchair production, in order to make it possible for every handicapped individual in the developing world to have access to a chair that is affordable, durable, and empowering. Their RoughRider wheelchair fulfills the group's mission through an open-source design that makes the end-user central during the production process.

RoughRider is a low-cost wheelchair that is optimized for the needs of users and the limitations of manufacturing facilities in developing countries. While most wheelchairs are designed to maneuver only on smooth surfaces, the RoughRider's wheels, frame, and mechanics make it suitable for more rugged conditions in both urban and rural areas, enabling the user to be independently mobile. The wheelchair is collapsible to fit in small spaces and includes functional features like low armrests, toe protectors for barefoot riding, a curvilinear frame to better fit the body and discourage the visual stigma of clunky chairs, and multiple rear axle positions to optimize stability. Its front set of smaller, caster-like wheels allow for increased durability, balance, and maneuverability over rough terrain. Its versatility enables a range of everyday activities including working, playing, traveling, going to school, and doing household chores. Additionally, its frame and components can all be assembled by anyone with basic manufacturing skills and materials. The need for parts, joints, and skilled labor is kept at a minimum to ensure both quality construction and easy maintenance.

To date, Whirlwind's technologies and designs have been used in 45 different countries, including by manufacturers in Colombia, India, Kenya, Mexico, Nicaragua, and Vietnam, to increase mobility and encourage community empowerment. Whirlwind continues to develop new technologies and has built a standards and testing branch within its organization to support the maintenance and sustainability of existing programs and products. The group, based at SFSU, also hosts a wheelchair design and construction class every semester for students and community members.

designer:
  Whirlwind Wheelchair
  International
other partners/clients/producers:
  Institute for Civic and Community
  Engagement at San Francisco
  State University (SFSU), local
  manufacturers
**geographical implementation/
market/availability:**
  Global, via independent
  manufacturers
status:
  Limited distribution
website:
  www.whirlwindwheelchair.org

Zipcar, Inc.

designers:
Robin Chase, Antje Danielson
geographical implementation/ market/availability:
Canada, UK, USA; via membership
status:
Consumer product
price:
$50 annual fee, plus usage plan
website:
www.zipcar.com

Zipcar is the world's largest car-sharing company and provider of on-demand vehicles. Its reliable and convenient network of shared cars provides an environmentally friendly, affordable alternative to owning an automobile. While cofounders Robin Chase and Antje Danielson were traveling in Berlin in 1999, they noticed that cars were available to the city's residents by the hour, eliminating the requirement for personal car ownership. Realizing this was an obvious and much-needed improvement to the lack of short-term car access in American cities, the duo launched the first Zipcar in Boston in 2000, followed soon after by fleets in Washington, D.C., and New York City. The cars in the system's fleet were equipped with wireless technology, allowing them to be rented through a user-friendly reservation system. Today tens of thousands of personal and business users rely on Zipcars in London, Vancouver, and dozens of US cities. Over 40 percent of Zipcar members have either sold their cars or delayed car purchases after joining the service. The company's fleet caters to all personal style preferences and capacity needs by including the hybrid Toyota Prius, MINI Coopers, and luxury and utility vehicles.

Potential users become Zipcar members by completing a basic application. They can then find locations near them for personal or business driving. (Many companies use Zipcar as an alternative to taxis, corporate vehicles, or travel rentals.) Members are issued a Zipcard, a key that is unique to them and that stores all personal information. Reservations are easily made using the company's online system, and vehicles can be reserved for one hour or up to four days. The chosen car waits at the selected location for the driver, who uses her Zipcard to unlock the vehicle. The key for the ignition is waiting inside the car, so she can then simply drive off. Drive time is billed by the hour or by the day, depending on the usage plan selected.

Zipcar's vision is to provide reliable and convenient access to on-demand transportation that complements other forms of mobility. The business's environmental impact is measurable: In cities serviced by the network, each Zipcar replaces more than 15 privately owned vehicles, and members report up to 50 percent reductions in their usual car usage. Some users report gas savings of over $5,000 per year, primarily because they plan trips more strategically when they have reserved a car for only a few hours. Zipcar continues to expand across the USA and internationally.

food

Adiri
Natural Nurser
Ultimate
Baby Bottle

With a less-than-subtle visual reference, the Adiri Natural Nurser Ultimate Baby Bottle sets a new standard for safe and user-friendly bottle-feeding. The product is comprised of three parts: the main vessel with nipple, a screw base, and a storage case. A Fill, Twist, and Feed system ensures quick meal preparation: The bottle is filled upside down, its cap is screwed to the bottom, and then it is ready for the child. Caregivers have found that this system makes the bottle easier to use, as compared to those that require plastic inserts or have small openings into which the liquid is poured. The Natural Nurser is free of bisphenol-A and polycarbonates, and a unique Petal vent helps reduce colic by facilitating the release of air from the vessel's interior. The bottle is dishwasher safe and comes in three stages that accommodate progressing flow rates.

The Natural Nurser resembles a breast as closely as possible in material and form for easy acceptance, particularly by babies hesitant to make the transition from breast-feeding to bottle-feeding. Its design is anthropomorphic yet simple, resulting in an intuitive and comfortable object for both caregiver and child.

Since its launch in 2000, Adiri has been an industry leader in creating products for feeding babies that promote happiness and health for both parents and children. The Natural Nurser is an update of the company's original product, the Breastbottle Nurser.

designer:
Whipsaw, Inc.
geographical implementation/ market/availability:
Global, via dealers
status:
Consumer product
price:
Approx. $12
website:
www.adiri.com

designer:
    Appropriate Infrastructure
    Development Group (AIDG)
geographical implementation/
market/availability:
    Global, on project basis
    through AIDG
status:
    Limited distribution
website:
    www.aidg.org

Alcohol Stoves

AIDG's Alcohol Stoves are a small-scale, cleaner alternative to the inefficient, high-emissions cooking techniques commonly used in the developing world. In these areas, AIDG supports the design and distribution of appropriate technologies that are locally made, inexpensive, and fulfill the basic needs of communities in innovative ways. Their compact stove has similar components to, and was inspired by, the ultra-efficient stoves used by backpackers. The device requires only basic materials including an aluminum soda can and cooking-grade alcohol, which burns much cleaner than charcoal or wood. The alcohol burns within the can, producing a flame that escapes through the vessel's pop-top opening to cook food placed above it. A shield made from a thin piece of aluminum or other malleable metal insulates the heat and protects the user from burns.

Through its other initiatives and with partner organizations, AIDG has distributed the stoves to communities in Guatemala and has helped develop a system there for the local production of grain and denatured alcohol for use as fuel. This integrated production process makes access to cooking alcohol local and affordable, while providing jobs and income for community members. Having a simple stove can help residents in this area significantly save on fuel costs, reduce emissions in their homes, and protect their families from burns.

BCK
Solar
Cooker

Unlike its large and cumbersome market competitors, the BCK Solar Cooker makes preparing food with the heat of the sun a portable and efficient process. The cooker is 10 inches (250 mm) tall and 5 inches (130 mm) in diameter, and since its only fuel source is direct sunlight, it is easily moved between locations.

The BCK has a flat reflective panel that, when its ends are joined, forms a cone. This shape and the product's heat-conducting material direct the sun's rays into the cone's center, where there is a black container filled with water. Depending on the sun's intensity, the water will reach a temperature of approximately 192 °F (90 °C). As it is heating, food is placed in the vessel and cooks there for about 45 minutes. To disassemble, the cone is collapsed and rolled into a smaller, cylindrical shape for compact storage. Thanks to its portability and ease of use, the BCK has applications for camping and outdoor excursions, as well as small-scale cooking in the developing world.

designers:
Javier Bertani, Ezequiel Castro,
Vera Kade
**geographical implementation/
market/availability:**
South America
status:
In development
websites:
www.bcksolar.com.ar
www.bck-id.com

Burr Mill

designer:
>Compatible Technology
>International (CTI)

**geographical implementation/
market/availability:**
>Global, through manufacturers in
>Uganda, USA, and Zimbabwe

status:
>Limited distribution

website:
>www.compatibletechnology.org

Because many of the world's poor survive on subsistence farming of less than 1 acre (0.4 ha) of land, the efficiency and sustainability of their crop harvesting is essential. CTI develops products and concepts that help families process harvested crops into nutritious food for consumption and storage throughout the dry season. The company's solutions to the problems of harvesting are safe, affordable, environmentally sensitive, and appropriate for local manufacturing technologies. Its Burr Mills include the Omega IV, Omega VI, and Ewing III models, which grind peanuts, grains, corn, coffee, or breadfruit into edible forms. The models operate with identical components but are optimized, based on labor and material availability, to be manufactured in three locations—Uganda, the USA, and Zimbabwe—for use around the world.

All models can be powered by hand-crank, bicycle, or electric motor and are made of common mechanical parts for easy local production. The system uses a thrust bearing, separate burrs to grind the food and remove the hulls of grains such as rice and wheat, and an auger shaft to pulverize the material. Thanks to its simplicity, the hand-crank is the most commonly employed operating means, but CTI has developed an instruction manual to help users adapt the tools into pedal-powered and engine-powered devices. Several hundred mills are currently in use, turning crops into usable forms for long-term storage and nutritious consumption.

Daily Dump

designers:
Poonam Bir Kasturi, Playnspeak
geographical implementation/ market/availability:
India, products via dealers, service via Daily Dump
status:
Consumer product
price:
Approx. $2.50–$25.00
website:
www.dailydump.org

Bangalore, India, produces 2,200 tons (1,996 T) of waste every day, but its central government's composting plant can only accommodate 500 tons (454 T) daily. Seventy percent of the waste generated in the average urban Indian home is organic wet waste, and most of Bangalore's houses have large garden areas as backyards. To address the waste issue and take advantage of the built-in space, designer Poonam Bir Kasturi created a one-stop shop for pots, tools, and services that delivers the benefits of aerobic composting to homes throughout India. Daily Dump is a composting brand, product, and service bundle that brings waste management to the home and empowers residents and new enterprises alike. By both educating people about composting and providing the products for the system, the company enables customers to take ownership of their household's waste management.

Users of the system purchase the earthenware pots from a wide selection: single or stacked, unpainted or

painted, individual or family capacity, indoor or outdoor, and even compost-and-plant pots. Customers can buy any combination of the vessels, along with tools and instruction material, to personalize the composting system to accommodate their needs. To complement the product range, Daily Dump offers weekly, biweekly, monthly, and emergency in-home service plans in which trained staff attend to pest maintenance, rotate waste, clean units, and more.

Daily Dump's open-source business model and product line also allow the pots to be replicated within craft communities throughout India. Through this design-meets-enterprise strategy, the company supports local workers while providing a solution to an urban environmental problem. "Design is a powerful tool that allows you to imagine a system that can be organic and enabling," asserts Kasturi.

GreenFire Technology Stoves

GreenFire Technology Stoves provide an economical, fuel-efficient, low-emission cooking option for homes and communities in the developing world, where the standard fuel utilized in kitchens can be costly and unhealthy. The stove's central feature is its ceramic combustion chamber made from lightweight aerated clay, which maximizes heat transfer, resulting in shorter cook times and the most effective use of fuel. The chamber is encased within metal housing for insulation and user safety.

Wood or charcoal is placed within the chamber, and a pot or pan sits on a metal stovetop that rests on the ceramic chamber. The stovetop, along with an angled "skirt" (an adjstable metal band) that is cinched around the perimeter of the pot, cradles the cooking vessel and forces the heat and gases up to the pot, ensuring that little warmth is lost. Simultaneously the chamber's clay serves as an insulating material and raises the internal air temperature, which results in more efficient burning. The combination of the chamber and skirt increases both heat transfer and combustion efficiency, producing an optimized, healthier method of cooking.

The technology is currently available in three models. The GreenFire One burns wood and is the top-performing one-door stove available for its price, while the GreenFire Two Combo is a two-door option that can burn wood or charcoal. The GreenFire Institutional Rocket Stove uses minimal wood to cook large quantities of food and vents emissions through a chimney.

designer:
Aprovecho Research Center
**geographical implementation/
market/availability:**
Global, via website
status:
Limited distribution
price:
$10–$30
websites:
www.aprovecho.org
www.stovetec.net

mesü

designer:
Studio Panepinto

**geographical implementation/
market/availability:**
Global, via dealers

status:
Consumer product

price:
$49.95 per set

website:
www.jenniferpanepinto.com

Mesü, a set of six porcelain nesting bowls, is a graceful tool for those trying to eat healthfully. The bowls range in size from .5 cup (120 ml) to 2 cups (480 ml) and measure portions with fill lines and colorful graphic systems that allow users to know exactly how much they are consuming. With this precision, the vessels can double as measuring cups in the kitchen, and the porcelain pieces are safe for use in the dishwasher, microwave, oven, and freezer. Beyond usability, the mesü bowls are beautiful as stand-alone objects. The set's sleek design conceals its dietary nature from anyone other than the user and thereby removes any embarrassment or taboo surrounding dieters' eating habits or portion requirements. The bowls have been utilized by diabetics, parents concerned with their children's weight, and general health-conscious eaters.

Short for "measure beautifully," mesü grew from Jennifer Panepinto's master's thesis at the School of Visual Arts in New York City, and was taken to market under the name Studio Panepinto. An active user of the bowls, Panepinto recounts, "After using them for so long, I really have a conscious awareness of how much food I am eating."

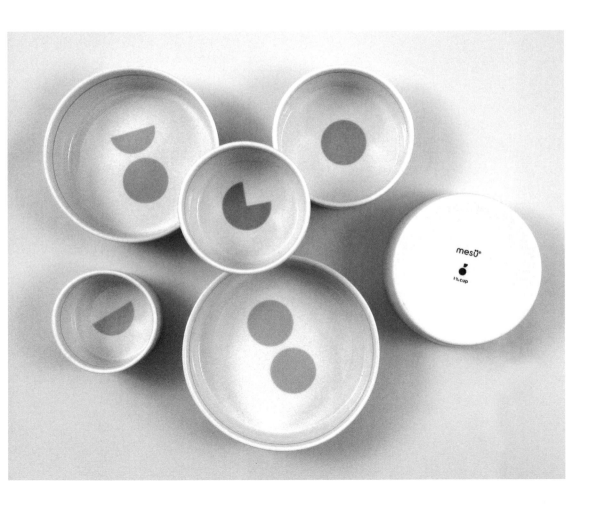

NatureMill

The NatureMill brings the composting process indoors. The system sits on a countertop or under a cabinet and is self-contained, odor-free, and automatic, requiring little maintenance and making it operable by even those with no prior knowledge of composting. Food waste of up to 120 pounds (55 kg) per month can be deposited into the NatureMill's upper chamber, where it is mixed, heated, moistened, and ventilated every four hours until it is ground into small particles. A fan constantly aerates the cultures, while a powerful carbon filter (which lasts for approximately five years) removes lingering odors. The material is then transferred through a trap door to the lower cure tray where it continues to compost while making space in the upper chamber for additional waste. The process is completed in two weeks, and a red light tells the user when to remove the compost for municipal collection or garden use.

For those without the time to commit to traditional compost systems, which can often involve frequent mixing, care, and monitoring, NatureMill is a simple alternative that requires about as much attention as a traditional trash can. The unit recycles its weight in waste every 10 days and uses just 5 kWh per month, less energy than the fuel that would be used by a garbage truck to move the same amount of trash.

designer:
NatureMill, Inc.
geographical implementation/ market/availability:
Global, via website and dealers
status:
Consumer product
price:
$299–$399
website:
www.naturemill.com

OXO
Good
Grips

designers:
Smart Design, OXO
**geographical implementation/
market/availability:**
USA, via dealers
status:
Consumer product
price:
$5–$40
website:
www.oxo.com

While watching his wife struggle with everyday tasks due to her painful arthritis, Sam Farber, a retired founder of a home goods company, saw an opportunity to create kitchen tools that were comfortable and easy to use for everyone. He came out of retirement and founded OXO, which since its inception in 1990 has grown into a large, well-respected kitchen and housewares brand known for thoughtful design that puts human needs first. The initial development of the company's product line, OXO Good Grips, was carried out by the firm Smart Design, with input from consumers, chefs, noted gerontologist Patricia Moore, and others. As a reminder of the line's design inspiration and the hands their products need to fit and serve, the staff at OXO's headquarters in New York collect and display gloves that they have found on the street.

The Good Grips product line now includes more than 750 tools for use in the kitchen, garden, and other areas of the home. Some of OXO's most popular items are its signature measuring cup that can be read from above, a salad spinner that can be used with one hand, a backlit oven thermometer that can be read through the oven window, and whistle-top teakettles with lids that open automatically when tipped. The company launches more than 50 new products each year, all of which aim to be "easiest to use for the largest possible spectrum of users." OXO's ability to fulfill this design mission and the company's commercial success prove that need-based, human-centered design is both functional and marketable.

Plumpy'nut

Many food supplements designed to fight malnutrition are devoid of flavor and disliked by the children who need them most. Nutriset, a France-based company dedicated to making products for malnourished populations in the developing world, created Plumpy'nut after realizing that children in almost every country like the taste of peanut butter. Made from a peanut base, the product delivers high nutritional value to the underfed. The ready-to-serve food is available in cups or sachets and has a nutritional profile similar to or better than that of F100 therapeutic milk, a common but more expensive foodstuff distributed in the developing world. A single 3.5-ounce (100-g) sachet provides over 500 calories and approximately 15 grams of protein. In 2006 more than 50,000 children in Ethiopia were treated for malnutrition with Plumpy'nut, and distribution has increased in the following years.

Plumpy'nut is produced by local franchises in the Democratic Republic of the Congo, Ethiopia, Malawi, and Niger, with planned expansions to factory partners in the Dominican Republic and other areas where malnutrition is a serious issue. Each franchise factory employs 15 to 70 local workers, which creates sustainable enterprises and new jobs. After the initial successful distribution of the supplement in Africa, Nutriset established the Plumpy'nut in the Field network to increase access to the product on local levels. Production of the supplement now occurs through one of two avenues: directly within the franchised producer's network, as in the case of Ethiopia's Hilina Enriched Food franchise, or through partnerships with community groups and NGOs. The latter tends to be smaller in scale, with the entities managed by social or humanitarian stakeholders to meet the needs of local nutritional programs and communities.

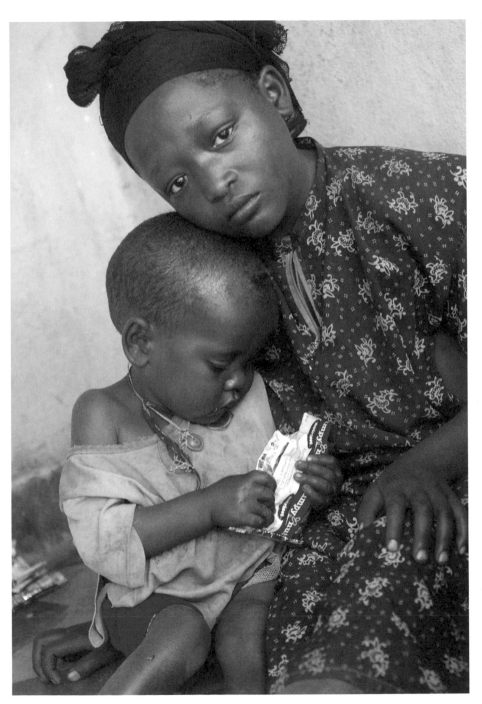

designer:
Nutriset
other partners/clients/producers:
Plumpy'nut in the Field franchise
network, International Medical
Corps (IMC)
**geographical implementation/
market/availability:**
Global, via franchises and field
projects
status:
Limited distribution
price:
Approx. $0.06 per package
website:
www.nutriset.fr

Sudanese
Refugee
Cookware

designer:
 Kristina Drury
**geographical implementation/
market/availability:**
 Sudan
status:
 Concept
website:
 Profile at www.coroflot.com

Due to ongoing political conflict and violence in Sudan, more than one-third of the country's citizens have been displaced from their homes and communities, and 2.8 million Sudanese refugees require food assistance annually. In refugee camps, cooking is difficult given restricted food supplies and insufficient wares to prepare meals. Oxfam provides refugees with flat-bottom pots, but reports within the camps show that most people sell those vessels in order to purchase round-bottom pots. This style of cookware is more accommodating of traditional twisting and cooking methods and easier to use with a "muswat," a crescent-shaped shell attached to a long stick designed for serving and stirring.

The tools created by Kristina Drury, an industrial design graduate student at Pratt Institute, address the needs, style, and culture of Sudanese cooking within the refugee camp context. The set, currently a concept, would pack into itself like Russian dolls and would include a variety of items: large and small lids for serving and cooking, four clear plastic cups for tea, handles for removing pots from the fire, a metal pitcher for serving tea, a kettle for heating water, small and large pots for cooking, and a metal bowl for serving. Pots and lids would be made from aluminum or steel through a stamping or casting process, and their prototypes were sized to fit within a stove that has been distributed in the camps and was designed by the Darfur Stoves Project. Cups would be made from durable clear plastic to visually resemble the traditional glass teacups used in Sudan. As a whole, the cookware set offers key benefits including ease of transport and manufacturing, full-service pieces for all kitchen needs, and systems that encourage kitchen safety to help prevent the burns that are commonly incurred when users remove pots from stoves.

Y Water

designer:
fuseproject
**geographical implementation/
market/availability:**
USA, via dealers
status:
Consumer product
price:
$1.69
website:
www.ywater.us

Although the overuse of plastic water bottles is hardly laudable, Y Water took advantage of the vessel's familiarity and made a bottle that is reusable and engaging to encourage good health and playtime creativity in children. The water itself is USDA-certified organic, preservative-free, sweetened with cane sugar, and enriched with nutrients. Each of its four flavors has a taste and name designed to appeal to kids and contains specific vitamins or minerals: Bone Water (calcium), Brain Water (zinc), Immune Water (vitamins A, C, and E), and Muscle Water (magnesium).

Once empty, the bottles transform from containers to building blocks using "Y Knot" connector pieces. The rubber connectors are available through Y Water and can be ordered online for only the price of shipping. With Y Knots, the bottles can be linked in a DNA-like manner, allowing kids to create structures resembling animals, robots, or anything in their imaginations.

Los Angeles–based Y Water pledges its environmental commitment by creating this second use for its product and distributing free mailers so its customers can send bottles directly to the company for recycling. The bottles are made from copolyester, a grade of durable plastic used in the medical industry and certified food-safe by the US Food and Drug Administration. They are free of harmful bisphenol-A and do not leach chemicals.

While the ubiquity of plastic water bottles raises issues of environmental sustainability, Y Water's approach and environmental focus extend the life of the bottle and foster nutrition and creativity in customers, hopefully encouraging happier and healthier children.

play

Boezels

designer:
Neo Human Toys

other partners/clients/producers:
The Wisselstroom Center

**geographical implementation/
market/availability:**
Global, via Neo Human Toys

status:
Limited distribution

website:
www.boezels.com

Designer Twan Verdonck of Neo Human Toys created Boezels as a multisensory form of therapy produced for and by the mentally challenged. The toys have also been used as anthropomorphic and engaging friends for the elderly, sufferers of Alzheimer's, and young children. Each of the 15 Boezels has characteristics that engage and excite specific senses. For example, the monkey, named Tummy, has a belly that can be warmed in the microwave to stimulate the sense of touch. The snake, Reura, has a relaxing aroma, while Tooh, the giant kangaroo, has a large pocket that the user can climb into. The rabbit, Tuttel, vibrates when its tail is pulled, and the zHumanoyd is an abstract baby whose mirrored face reflects its owner's image. In combination, Boezels create safe, engaging learning environments for children and adults with mental disabilities.

Though each has a specific form, the Boezels are collectively rooted in their tactile and therapeutic qualities. Each toy encourages contact and physical engagement between user and object and stimulates the sense of touch for the mentally challenged, who find emotional and physical comfort through this act of play. Varying in size from 8 inches to 80 inches (20 cm to 200 cm), each Boezel is handmade using fake furs and textured fabrics by members of The Wisselstroom Center, a day care facility for the mentally challenged in The Netherlands. "My project is a metaphor and example for how we could deal with social care, industry, design, and art," explains Verdonck.

DIY Soccer Balls

designers:
   Liza Forester, Martí Guixé,
   and others
**geographical implementation/
market/availability:**
   Global
status:
   DIY
price:
   Cost of materials, $18 for tape
website:
   www.guixe.com

Soccer is the most widely played sport in the world. On manicured lawns in California, dirt patches in rural Uganda, or the professional fields of the European leagues, soccer has become something of an international language.

Like the sport itself, the manner in which soccer balls are designed and manufactured is also diverse, ranging from the highly inspected, top-quality leather World Cup balls to do-it-yourself versions. In the developing world, it is common for children to make soccer balls from layers of plastic bags wrapped within each other; a condom stuffed with paper, plastic, or cloth; or a single bag stuffed with other waste and tied off tightly. Some DIY soccer ball designs have been leveraged into viable business enterprises, creating jobs for stitchers through local production (see Alive & Kicking, p. 274). All DIY soccer balls represent a design achievement in bringing the sport to children who otherwise wouldn't have access to it. However, two of the most interesting developments in this

market are designs by Liza Forester and Martí Guixé.

Forester, a student at Parsons the New School for Design, focused on the creation of a sustainable enterprise in the development of her thesis concept project, Let's Kick It. The project provides African women and orphaned girls afflicted by AIDS with patterns to stitch fabric soccer balls that are then stuffed with plastic bags and sold. The Let's Kick It project was developed in partnership with UNICEF and Key Club International's "Kick HIV/AIDS out of Kenya" program.

Catalonian designer Guixé took a cheeky approach to his DIY design, producing a tape that is printed with a soccer ball pattern and wrapped around a ball of paper or plastic bags. (He says the "tape ball" works best when stuffed with sports magazines.) The tape is mass-produced but relies on user engagement, creating a light-hearted dialogue that allows players to have fun making their own toys that still have the recognizable aesthetic of traditional soccer balls.

Regardless of location, material, scale, or cost, a DIY soccer ball is a great example of individual creativity. It represents a user's personal investment in a global pastime and the ingenuity sometimes required to bring play into one's own life.

Foldschool

Everyday materials, free open-source design, and direct engagement with the user make Foldschool an accessible model for toy and furniture design. Developed by Swiss architect and designer Nicola Enrico Stäubli, Foldschool is a collection of plans for cardboard furniture for kids. Plans are downloaded from Stäubli's website and handcrafted by the user. The patterns for a stool, chair, and rocker are intended to be assembled by both parent and child, and can be printed on letter-sized paper using any standard printer. Additional tools required include a pair of scissors, ruler, spray-fix adhesive, craft glue, and tape.

Each fragment of the pattern is printed on its own sheet of paper and cut out. The individual fragments are assembled into the full-sized master pattern, which is spray-fixed to a large piece of cardboard. The user then cuts the cardboard along the pattern's edges and folds it along the dotted lines. A step-by-step construction manual on the designer's website has additional instructions for gluing the

folded pieces together to fully form the corners and joints of each piece of furniture.

"Mass culture is run by superficiality and ecological absurdity," states Stäubli. "Foldschool supports craftsmanship as a face-to-face approach to design and brings together product and user [as closely as] possible." The patterns represent open-source design at its best, making the user a co-designer and relying on human craft and interaction with the materials for construction.

designer:
Nicola Enrico Stäubli
**geographical implementation/
market/availability:**
Global, via website
status:
DIY
price:
Cost of materials
website:
www.foldschool.com

Game for the Masses

designer:
 Futurefarmers
other partners/clients/producers:
 Jack Hanley Gallery
status:
 Project implemented
website:
 www.futurefarmers.com

Game for the Masses was a research project by San Francisco–based art and design group Futurefarmers that was installed at the Jack Hanley Gallery in San Francisco in 2002. The game board, measuring 4 by 4 feet (1.2 m) square and made from wood, tape, paper, and string, was created to allow the designers to observe social interactions around gaming. Over the course of the one-evening event, it revealed how people use games as an interface through which they relate, exchange, and interact.

The installation included a set of rules and instructions but left much to be interpreted and customized by the players. Throughout the event, participants developed multiplayer, three-dimensional, gambling, and architectural versions of the game.

page 250
Design Revolution
play

The game included the following:

Contents
One game board, 14 one-slot pucks, eight two-hole pucks, one 14-inch (36-cm) string, one polyhedron die

Set-Up
Distribute pucks equally among players

Number of Players
Two to four

Game Objective
To obtain all pucks

Default Rules
Areas outside of red boxes are out of bounds

How to Play
Choose a player to go first. Each player places a puck of his choice on the board in the main rectangle, which is defined by red tape. The first player rolls the die into the rectangle attempting to land on a puck. If a puck is touched by the die, the player gets to take the puck into his possession. If the player does not touch a puck, he must put one of his pucks on the board. A rectangle on the left is a community pool or gambling area. There is also a string hanging from the ceiling; however, no rules are assigned to it.

Suggestions
If you create chains with the pucks, a player may have the chance to win several pucks.

While Game for the Masses was a research-based exploration that took place during a one-time event, the experience choreographed by the game's set-up and instructions draws interesting parallels between design and play. The designers' attention to aesthetic elements and the game's rules brought playful interaction to a social setting, revealing human instincts to compete with others and engage with physical surroundings.

GIANTmicrobes

In 2002 young attorney Drew Oliver gave up his law practice and followed an entrepreneurial impulse. The career shift resulted in GIANTmicrobes, a line of softball-sized, plush toys that resemble real microbes, ranging from the common cold to the Ebola virus, at one million times their actual size. Each toy comes with an image of, and information about, the microbe it depicts. Categories include Infirmaries (chicken pox, pneumonia), Maladies (bad breath, athlete's foot), Calamities (black death, flesh-eating virus), Exotics (bacteria discovered within a Mars rock), and Critters (bed bugs, dust mites).

The toys can be silly gifts perfect for a sick child, but more than that, their literal magnification of the unseen has proven to be an interesting tool for health education through the company's Professional Series for public health and institutional applications. The line began after Oliver was approached by medical authorities who desired a more engaging way to convey information about diseases

that are a threat to public health. The products, which include HIV, hepatitis, TB, and polio toys, have since been effectively integrated into small- and large-scale health programs for children and adults. Playful and non-language-specific, GIANTmicrobes can be used by people of all ages and in all countries.

designer:
Giantmicrobes, Inc.
geographical implementation/ market/availability:
Global, via website and dealers
status:
Consumer product
price:
$7.95
website:
www.giantmicrobes.com

H-racer

Until full-sized hydrogen cars become a viable and affordable form of transportation, the H-racer will have to suffice. Developed by Horizon Fuel Cell Technologies, whose mission is "to greatly accelerate the global commercialization of clean, hydrogen fuel cell power," the 6.3-by-2.8-by-1.8-inch (16-by-7-by-4.5-cm) H-racer is a toy car entirely powered by hydrogen. Using its fuel cell and on-board storage system, the miniature H-Racer can propel itself over 328 feet (100 m). The car comes with its own solar-powered hydrogen refueling station, or the user can simply add water to the station's tank to produce new fuel.

Most of the discussion about hydrogen vehicles centers on the science and technology, but the H-racer injects a bit of fun into the quest for renewable fuel sources. Through play, the tiny, zero-emissions car teaches the advantages of hydrogen fuel: It is nontoxic, renewable, clean burning, and made from the most abundant element on the planet.

designer:
Horizon Fuel Cell Technologies
geographical implementation/ market/availability:
Global, via website and dealers
status:
Consumer product
price:
$100
website:
www.horizonfuelcell.com

jive

designer:
Ben Arent
**geographical implementation/
market/availability:**
UK
status:
In development
website:
jive.benarent.co.uk

Jive is a three-part networking interface that brings digital social interactions to an unexpected market: grandparents and the elderly. Designed by Ben Arent as his undergraduate industrial design project at Middlesex University, jive was inspired by observation of the elderly as a community, particularly their disconnectedness from technology-based networking. The desktop portal addresses the social needs of this often technophobic demographic, allowing grandparents to stay connected with friends and family members and meet new people by creating profiles and posting and receiving updates. Jive combines a large, graphics-based monitor named Betty, "Friend Passes," and a one-plug router to mitigate the major technological frustrations that the elderly most commonly report. The router is preloaded with ISP settings for a true plug-and-play experience. Betty, the monitor, is a tangible user interface that does not require a mouse and relies on large photos and images rather than small type, which can be difficult

for the elderly to read.

Perhaps the most unique feature of jive is the Friend Pass, a radio frequency identification tag that gives user profiles a concrete form. Much like a business card, users exchange Friend Passes, then connect them to the dock in the jive monitor to immediately upload that person's information and digitally connect to her updates, photographs, and additional information.

Kidsonroof House

Though its architecture and styling can vary greatly, the dollhouse is a near universal object of play. Dutch company Kidsonroof has refined the traditional dollhouse into its most basic form, a white cardboard home, simultaneously simplifying an iconic toy and creating a world of possibilities. Kidsonroof House, the aptly named structure, can be occupied by small children and has few built-in features—only windows, doors, and a letterbox—its white cardboard structure begging to be drawn upon, pasted, colored, and decorated. The play space (47 by 28 by 34 inches [120 by 71 by 86 cm]) is packed and shipped flat, facilitating easy storage for years to come. Whether used as a dollhouse, safe haven, fortress, castle, or hiding place from monsters, House is a blank canvas for children's imaginations. Kidsonroof donates five percent of its profits to UNICEF projects, including small-scale housing for orphans suffering from HIV/AIDS in Russia.

designer:
Kidsonroof
other partners/clients/producers:
UNICEF
geographical implementation/
market/availability:
Global, via website
status:
Consumer product
price:
Approx. $45
website:
www.kidsonroof.com

LEGO Mindstorms

LEGO Mindstorms is a line of electronically enabled parts and kits that combines creativity and technology in robotic form. The latest Mindstorm robots, the NXT generation, can be built in 30 minutes and integrate traditional LEGO blocks with a 32-bit microprocessor, motor parts, and light, sound, and visual sensors. Like all Mindstorm kits, NXT allows users to engage in the design and construction of a working robot and to understand the electronic components as enhancing elements.

The Mindstorm sets provide endless opportunities for design, experimentation, and open-sourced creation. Robots can be built in various forms and embedded with different commands to execute particular actions based on the user's preferences. The Accelerometer Sensor, for example, tells the robot which way is up, right, and left, providing three axes for measuring its motion, acceleration, and g-forces (for jet fighter or astronaut simulation). Programs for actions can be wirelessly downloaded to the robot, while Bluetooth technology makes NXT robots controllable by remote devices such as a mobile phone or PDA.

Mindstorm kits have been used in school programs, corporate settings, universities, and more. An online community of Mindstorm enthusiasts supports the open-source platform by sharing information, posting photographs to galleries, and recommending best practices.

In developing Mindstorms, Danish designers Pelle Norman Petersen, Jørn K. Thomsen, and Tine Vangsbo sought to create a technologically innovative system that was intuitive, relevant, and engaging, but that could be understood and used by a wide market. Despite the technological components, Mindstorm is rooted in design that facilitates a creative experience between object and user. By approaching the system from both a playful and a high-tech perspective, the designers were able to create a full-service toy kit that caters to a range of skill levels while combining education and recreation.

designers:
Pelle Norman Petersen, Jørn K. Thomsen, Tine Vangsbo
other partners/clients/producers:
LEGO
geographical implementation/ market/availability:
Global, via website or dealers
status:
Consumer product
price:
Up to $250
website:
mindstorms.lego.com

Nike + iPod Sport Kit

The Nike + iPod Sport Kit connects shoe to gadget, using an iPod to monitor a runner's fitness performance while he is jogging to a personalized soundtrack. Nike+ shoes have built-in pockets beneath their insoles that hold a piezoelectric accelerometer sensor, and a receiver attaches to an iPod nano or iPod touch. The sensor monitors movement and converts that motion into usable data. As the user runs, information about his speed, distance, and calories burned is sent to the iPod, where it can be viewed and tracked. Audio feedback updates the user on workout progression, and prerecorded congratulations from world-class athletes Lance Armstrong, Tiger Woods, and others give added encouragement when a runner achieves a personal best or reaches a long-term milestone.

The system also allows for custom workouts catered to a user's needs and routines. Workout sessions can be defined by time, distance, or calorie goals, and are then set to an iPod playlist or song selection for personalized motivation. After working out, the user can connect the iPod to a Mac or PC computer, which syncs the workout data through an online interface at www.nikeplus.com for further tracking or information sharing with other runners worldwide.

The partnership between the companies, leaders within their respective industries, represents a symbiotic brand collaboration that enhances both the individual product offerings and the user experience.

Fits in your Nike+ shoe   Plugs into your iPod nano

NIKE + iPod

designers:
   NIKE, Inc., Apple
**geographical implementation/
market/availability:**
   Global, via website or dealers
status:
   Consumer product
price:
   $29, iPod and shoes not included
websites:
   www.apple.com
   www.nike.com

odo

designer:
Sony Corp.
status:
Concept
website:
www.sony.net

In 2006 Sony developed prototypes for odo, a suite of toys that are powered by kinetic energy and intended to encourage curiosity, creativity, and energy in play. The project was one of Sony's corporate sustainability initiatives that explored issues of social and environmental responsibility among the company, its products, and its consumers.

The five gadgets in the odo line are: the Crank N' Capture video camera, powered by a handle on its side to shoot and play back images in a flip-book effect; the Spin N' Snap digital camera, powered by sticking one's fingers through the camera's two holes and spinning the device end over end; the Push Power Play photo and video viewer, powered by pressing the gadget's bottom-mounted roller; the Pull N' Play stereo headphones, powered by pulling an attached cord; and the Juice Box solar battery, which collects sunlight when it is stuck to a window with its attached suction cups. After charging, the Juice Box can be used as a portable battery for other odo toys. The simple, unadorned forms of the gadgets speak to users on a basic level, encouraging self-expression and individual interactions with the objects and the physical world in general.

While the odo line has not yet been mass-produced, it served as an internal exercise for Sony to explore user engagement and human motion as a renewable energy source. The odo toys combine childlike curiosity with high-tech gadgets and represent a playful form of consumerism that is simultaneously marketable and socially conscious.

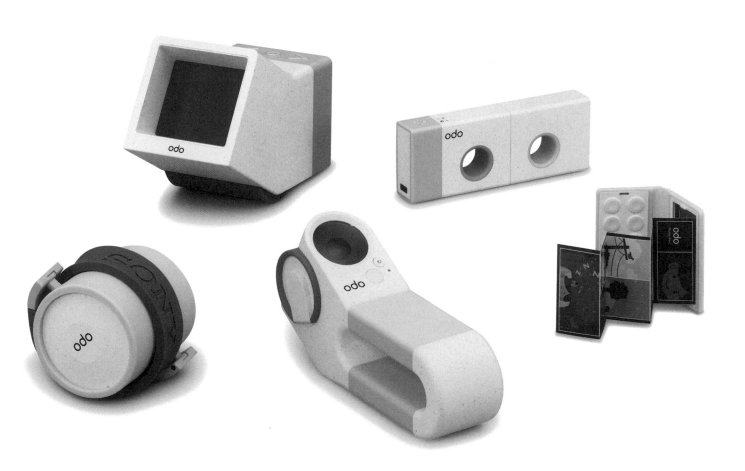

PicoCricket

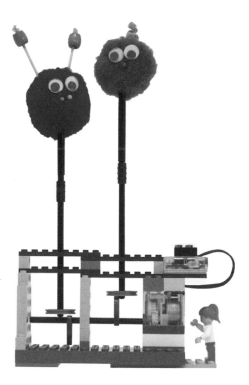

The PicoCricket invention kit combines simple technologies and artistic expression. PicoCricket itself is a tiny computer that, when connected to other parts in the kit, makes things light up, play music, and spin, enabling children to design and build unique toys and gadgets. The kit comes with the small computer, electronic components, craft materials, and suggestions for projects. The electronic components include a motor, motor board, sound box, light "beamer," colored lights, LED digital display, and sound, light, and touch sensors. Each component, when connected to the PicoCricket computer and integrated into an artistic project, creates lively and interactive objects for creative learning and play. For example, a child could make a dog from the craft materials and embed the touch sensor and sound box inside to make the dog bark when it is petted.

Children can use the parts to invent creations that range from kinetic sculptures to magic lanterns, all with light, sound, and visual features.

Teachers can also find additional workshop and instructional ideas on PicoCricket's website, which encourages curricular applications. Though it relies on technological elements, the system facilitates easy creation through simple wire components and familiar craft pieces.

PicoCricket was designed by Smart Design and PICO, which develops new technologies and activities that engage children in creative learning experiences through expression, experimentation, and exploration. The kit blurs the line between play and education, encouraging learning through creation, tactility, and simultaneous technological and artistic explorations.

designers:
Smart Design, Playful Invention Company, Inc. (PICO)

other partners/clients/producers:
Massachusetts Institute of Technology (MIT) Media Lab, LEGO

geographical implementation/ market/availability:
Global, via website

status:
Consumer product

price:
$250 per set

website:
www.picocricket.com

Playground Fence

designers:
Tejo Remy, René Veenhuizen
other partners/clients/producers:
De Noorderlicht Primary School
**geographical implementation/
market/availability:**
Dordrecht, The Netherlands
status:
Project implemented
website:
www.remyveenhuizen.nl

Dutch designers Tejo Remy and René Veenhuizen are known for their clever designs that encourage new user experiences and create connections between people and objects. When commissioned in 2004 to transform the playground space at the primary school De Noorderlicht in Dordrecht, The Netherlands, their goal was to inspire new interactions while adding no new material to the space. With those objectives in mind, they looked to the existing infrastructure of the school's standard metal fence as an opportunity. Remy and Veenhuizen reimagined it not as a two-dimensional barrier, but as a three-dimensional, inhabitable space that would create new experiences for students and passersby on either side of it. By altering the shape of the vertical fence, adding convex and concave curves to the bars, the designers created meeting places, seating, and play spaces within its structure. Distortions to the traditional rhythm of the fence yield new geometries that are both aesthetically appealing and functional.

As a result, the fence becomes a part of the playground for the children rather than an exclusionary element, and provides an opportunity for parents and other community members to engage with students.

page 270
Design Revolution
play
+ education

Tessera

designer:
Christian John
other partners/clients/producers:
Inter-Agency Network for
Education in Emergencies,
International Rescue Committee
**geographical implementation/
market/availability:**
Iraq, Jordan, Syria
status:
Concept
website:
www.design21sdn.com/
share/1915

Since the US-led invasion of Iraq in 2003, violence and chaos have forced Iraqi families out of their homes and communities and into other areas of the country or refugee camps in neighboring Jordan and Syria. Often this turmoil most affects the displaced children, who suffer from a lack of identity and stable education. Tessera, an interactive educational game for young Iraqi refugees, attempts to teach problem-solving skills, encourage the communication of personal experiences, and rejuvenate identity and cultural pride at a moment when children are searching for a sense of home and personal roots.

The earthenware puzzle was Christian John's thesis project at Parsons the New School for Design. Made from clay, a common yet precious material in the region, Tessera can be locally produced and has a tactile familiarity for youngsters. The game focuses on three principles particular to refugee children's educational needs: cognitive development, expression as a form of trauma therapy, and community participation in the recalling of cultural and historical heritage.

The puzzle uses words, colors, and shapes and is designed to be played by a group. Tessera's central, star-shaped piece is first to be placed in the area of play, and the remaining pieces are distributed among participants. Edges of the pieces are painted blue, green, yellow, or purple, to indicate placement in relation to the other parts. Each child takes a turn placing her shape where it fits in the puzzle. Some pieces are cues for storytelling and are inscribed with words that make reference to issues of Iraqi identity, history, community, and heritage. When one of these pieces is played, one or more children tell a story or share a memory that relates to the term. The game continues until the puzzle is complete. The process fosters relationship building and cooperation as a group to construct a central object.

enterprise

Alive & Kicking

Alive & Kicking is a UK-based charity that makes inexpensive, durable, repairable sports balls using labor and leather local to the areas in Africa where the products are distributed. Each soccer ball, netball, or volleyball is printed with an informative message about HIV/AIDS, malaria, or TB treatment or prevention. To date, Alive & Kicking has employed over 150 workers in Kenya, South Africa, and Zambia, who have produced and distributed over 200,000 balls to schools, orphanages, slums, and refugee camps throughout Africa.

The sports balls cross cultures to unite youth through play. Soccer remains the most popular sport in the world, with children across Africa playing from a young age through adulthood. Because the balls are printed with disease information, they become platforms for health education for teachers, community members, and parents, who can employ a familiar and beloved object to educate children. Additionally, the balls can be returned to the organization for repair, providing a long life for the products and ongoing income for stitchers.

The charity has three primary goals: distribute sports balls to kids to encourage play and fitness; educate children about the dangers of HIV/AIDS, malaria, and TB; and provide new jobs to unemployed adults, paying them a fair wage for their stitching work. Local stitchers produce up to three balls each day, accounting for a total of approximately 7,000 balls from three factories each month. The finished products are distributed through donations from individuals, organizations, corporations, and governments.

Alive & Kicking has also partnered with other charity projects, including Balls into Africa 2010, which hopes to distribute 100,000 sports balls to the poorest children in sub-Saharan Africa in time for the 2010 World Cup, and the Great Football Giveaway, which worked to donate 2,000 balls to communities in Zambia. The group also hosted then Senator Barack Obama, who visited the Kenyan factory to learn more about the organization.

designer:
    Alive & Kicking
other partners/clients/producers:
    Various Africa- and UK-based
    NGOs
**geographical implementation/
market/availability:**
    Africa, by donation
status:
    Limited distribution
price:
    $15 per ball
website:
    www.aliveandkicking.org.uk

designers:
    Artecnica, commissioned
    designers
**geographical implementation/
market/availability:**
    Global, via dealers
status:
    Consumer product
price:
    $50–$1,000
website:
    www.artecnicainc.com

Design with Conscience

Artecnica, a design company based in Los Angeles, "blends art and technology to elevate the purpose and value of everyday objects by using design to enchant, inspire, and transform." More than only making aesthetic statements, Artecnica's products integrate stories and craft and create an engagement between person and object. In particular, the company's award-winning Design with Conscience product line brings traditional craft to a high-design market in enterprise-supporting, sustainable ways.

Each item is the result of a collaboration between a world-renowned designer and an artisan community. Through the art direction overseen by Artecnica, artisans and designers are paired and work together directly throughout the development process, creating products that showcase design talent and traditional handcraft. Eco-friendly local materials and production methods ensure environmental and social sustainability. Best-selling items include Dutch designer Hella Jongerius's Beads and Pieces, a four-piece ceramic collection hand shaped by a potter community in Peru, and the Brazilian Campana brothers' transNeomatic, a set of bowls made from artfully woven rattan and repurposed tires by the skilled Hai Tai weavers of rural Vietnam. By creating "luxury" design pieces through the traditional production methods of craft communities, Artecnica empowers grassroots enterprises while supporting emerging design talent.

Donation Meter Program

designer:
Denver's Road Home

other partners/clients/producers:
Campaign to End Homelessness,
City of Denver, Community
Appeals Advisory Board,
Denver Department of Public
Works, Downtown Denver
Partnership, Leadership Denver,
Mayor John Hickenlooper,
Mile High United Way, OZ
Architecture, rabble+rouser

**geographical implementation/
market/availability:**
Denver, Colorado

status:
Project implemented

website:
www.denversroadhome.org

A study conducted by the City of Denver found that citizens gave $4.5 million per year directly to homeless panhandlers, with 99 percent of those donations then going toward drug and alcohol purchases. Denver's Road Home, an organization leading the Campaign to End Homelessness, partnered with individuals, institutions, and the Denver city government to propose a solution to this problem that engaged citizens while reallocating donations toward counseling, transportation, food, shelter, and job-training programs for those in need. The result was the Donation Meter Program, which serves as a middleman between donations and aid to the homeless. The program uses nonfunctioning parking meters as donation "piggy banks," where individuals can deposit spare change. The collections go directly to the Mile High United Way to fund predetermined programs to benefit the homeless population.

The program began in March 2007 with the installation of 36 repurposed standard city meters in stra-tegic downtown locations that had both existing panhandling issues and significant foot traffic. Within the first month, 16,411 coins, totaling $2,000, were donated. The initial success led to a second installation of 50 refurbished meters in September 2007. Each of the meters is painted bright red and has "Denver's Road Home" printed on it, along with information and graphics that outline the impact a donation will make: $0.50 helps a homeless person ride public transportation, $1.50 buys a meal, and $20 provides a homeless family with shelter, clothing, employment assistance, and government case management for one day. (The meters only accept coins, but larger donations may be made through the organization's website.) With the 86 existing meters, the program's organizers anticipate donations of $100,000 per year in coin contributions and sponsorships. In the future, Denver's Road Home, the Mile High United Way, and the Department of Public Works plan to maintain existing locations and coordinate

sponsorships for additional meters.

The donation program is part of Denver's Road Home's greater campaign, the Ten-Year Plan to End Homelessness, and is a humanitarian application of design thinking toward a sustainable and structured public program. "The Donation Meter demonstrates yet another innovative way in which this community is responding to Denver's Road Home and our commitment to ending homelessness," says Mayor John Hickenlooper. Thanks to this and the city's other homeless programs, in December 2007 Denver reported an 11 percent reduction in the homeless population, along with a 36 percent decrease in chronic homelessness.

Freecycle
Network

designers:
Deron Beal, The Freecycle Network
geographical implementation/ market/availability:
Global, via website
status:
Project implemented
website:
www.freecycle.org

From its humble origins in Tucson, Arizona, The Freecycle Network has become the world's largest environmental web community, with over 5.7 million members in more than 85 countries. Its premise is simple: connect local people and neighborhoods through the exchange of free goods. More specifically, the Freecycle mission is to "build a worldwide gifting movement that reduces waste, saves precious resources, and eases the burden on our landfills, while enabling our members to benefit from the strength of a larger community."

Begun by Deron Beal in 2003 with an e-mail to approximately 40 friends, Freecycle uses the Yahoo! Groups network to connect people to free furniture, housewares, bicycles, and other objects. All goods must be offered for free with no strings attached. The "offer-and-take" structure is clean and simple and is effectively the most efficient form of recycling, cutting out intermediate parties and transferring ownership of goods to give them a second life in a new home.

To join the network, a user signs up for her local Freecycle Yahoo! Group. If she has an object to offer or is in need of something, she sends an e-mail or posts a message via the group website, listing her location and the item she is getting rid of or looking to acquire. Intergroup correspondence follows, connecting offers to needs. The transferring of goods between the two parties is arranged. Each city or local group has a moderator to oversee the network and tend to administrative tasks.

Freecycle is run by over 10,000 volunteers worldwide, who estimate that "freecycling" keeps approximately 300 tons (272 t) of trash out of landfills every day, for a total of 400 million pounds (181 million kg)—a heap five times the height of Mount Everest—in the last year. Each week an average of 40,000 new members join the group.

The free offerings are not only environmentally friendly but also a gesture of gift-giving that has significant social impact, creating interactions between individuals that might not otherwise occur and reallocating resources in meaningful, need-based ways. A Louisville, Kentucky, freecycler shares, "I gave a loveseat to a lady who had nothing. Her husband had walked out on her and her children, and they were starting over from scratch. She was so thankful she cried—over a loveseat I would have probably thrown away."

The power of Freecycle is not its web presence but the real-world action it facilitates. The group is only as successful as its in-person transferring of goods, making it a unique form of social networking that translates online relationships into real-world exchanges and experiences.

FreeRice

partners/clients/producers:
Berkman Center for Internet and Society at Harvard University, United Nations' World Food Program, Poverty.com
geographical implementation/ market/availability:
Global, via website
status:
Project implemented
website:
www.freerice.com

FreeRice is an organization and online experience that simultaneously educates visitors to its website and helps curtail world hunger by giving rice to those who need it. At www.freerice.com, each visitor is prompted to play a vocabulary game; for every question answered correctly, 10 grains of rice are donated to United Nations World Food Program initiatives. In essence, the site lets you learn new words or subject-based trivia while feeding the hungry.

On the site, players are given a word and must select its definition from multiple-choice answers. Versions of the game focused on subjects including chemistry, geography, and languages are also available. Difficulty levels are automatically adjusted as questions are progressively answered correctly or incorrectly. As answers are recorded, a graphic bowl of rice on the right of the screen displays how many grains a player has successfully donated.

As an enterprise, FreeRice uses web traffic for two good causes: providing free education and creating a philanthropic solution to a global problem. While it is a small amount, 10 grains of rice is a graspable quantity that makes giving personal. College students, CEOs, and children alike have enjoyed the site's vocabulary-building games. In its first year in existence, FreeRice players donated enough rice to feed more than two million people in Bangladesh, Cambodia, Myanmar, Uganda, and beyond.

Futurelab

partners/clients/producers:
Policy, industry, research, and educational institutions
geographical implementation/ market/availability:
UK, on project basis
status:
Project implemented
website:
www.futurelab.org.uk

Bringing cutting-edge innovation to the classroom, UK-based Futurelab engages in research, development, partnerships, and testing to enhance learning experiences through interactive technologies and interfaces. "We need to nurture a generation of creative learners capable of dealing with the immense challenges of this century," explains David Puttnam, Futurelab's chairman. The nonprofit organization works in partnership with myriad institutions, schools, designers, and engineers to develop interactive games and learning systems. Futurelab's team of researchers incubates new ideas and develops them from concepts to fleshed-out prototypes, moving them from lab to classroom. The group shares best practices and hard evidence, communicates the latest educational thinking, and hosts events to exchange ideas in a collaborative arena to foster broader implementation and support of similar tools.

Projects to date have included Newtoon, a cell phone and web game embedded with physics lessons and designed in partnership with Soda Creative, and Fountaineers, a system created with Stakeholder Design for an outdoor school fountain whose purpose, programming, use, and maintenance will be decided and executed by the students. Futurelab is a unique meeting place for the creative, educational, and technological sectors to build sustainable and socially innovative solutions for the next generation of leaders and thinkers.

Grameen Danone

Grameen Danone is a social enterprise whose mission is to reduce poverty and bring health to children through food using a community-based business model. The partnership was agreed upon with a handshake over a casual lunch meeting in 2005 between Muhammad Yunus, winner of the Nobel Peace Prize and founder of the Bangladesh-based Grameen Bank (known as "the bank of the poor"), and Franck Riboud, chief executive of the French food company Groupe Danone. The seemingly unexpected alignment of the two companies proves the value of socially sustainable businesses that can apply innovative corporate models to basic human needs. The agreement follows Yunus's original proposal: The two entities would work together to address the food needs of children in the developing world and recoup only their original investment and a one percent profit, reinvesting the rest into the enterprise.

In November 2006, Grameen Danone launched its first product, a yogurt called Shoktidoi, designed to nourish Bangladeshi children at an affordable price point, just 5 BDT (about $0.08). Shoktidoi, which is made from cow's milk and molasses from dates, compensates for nutritional deficiencies, delivering calcium, protein, vitamins, minerals, and micronutrients.

The yogurt is produced at the Bogra, Bangladesh, plant, which is Grameen Danone's first facility and will serve as a prototype for future locations. The goals for the plants are to create as many jobs as possible within the surrounding community, use minimum machinery to promote full-time workers, and create a supply chain with microfarms that provide raw materials such as milk, sugar, and molasses. The local farmers are also eligible for microloans from Grameen Bank to support or expand their businesses. Grameen Danone products are distributed based on the "Grameen Ladies" system, in which small wholesalers sell the product door-to-door, currently providing

designers:
Franck Riboud (Groupe Danone), Muhammad Yunus (Grameen Bank)

other partners/clients/producers:
Global Alliance for Improved Nutrition

geographical implementation/ market/availability:
Bangladesh, via dealers and Grameen Ladies

status:
Limited distribution

websites:
www.danone.com
www.grameen-info.org

more than 1,600 people in Bangladesh with jobs and additional income. The Grameen Danone enterprise is part of a new momentum of socially oriented, for-profit business ventures that equate financial and social value. The partnership places concern for people at the heart of its business model, creating jobs and increasing individual and environmental health.

"This represents a unique initiative in creating a social business enterprise, i.e., an enterprise not to maximize profit, but created with a declared mission to maximize benefits to the people served without incurring losses," observes Yunus. "It is a small project to begin with, but contains the seed of a new breed of business, which can change the economic world fundamentally. World famous Danone's participation in it, and Danone chairman Franck Riboud's presence in Dhaka, [Bangladesh], shows very clearly that this is not a fancy idea, but a serious business— business to make a difference in the world."

Keep the
Change

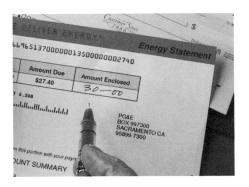

designer:
    IDEO
other partners/clients/producers:
    Bank of America
**geographical implementation/
market/availability:**
    USA, via Bank of America website
    and branches
status:
    Project implemented
website:
    www.bankofamerica.com

One of Bank of America's account offerings, Keep the Change, helps its customers save money with ease. Any customer with linked checking and savings accounts can enroll in the program. Each time a user pays for something with his Bank of America check card, the purchase is rounded up to the nearest dollar, and the difference is transferred from his checking to his savings account. For example, if a bag of groceries costs $21.47, that value is rounded to $22.00, $21.47 paying for the groceries and $0.53 moving from the checking to the savings account. By making it virtually effortless, Bank of America helps customers save more, while the institution benefits from opening more accounts. Additionally, the save-while-spending tactic does not disrupt consumers' habits and integrates a fiscally responsible service into the act of spending.

While the program, conceptualized by IDEO, is less product design than a thoughtful service offering, it demonstrates creative thinking that is beneficial for both business and customer and is rooted in human factors. Less than one year after launching Keep the Change, Bank of America opened 700,000 new checking accounts and one million new savings accounts, helping individual users save hundreds or even thousands of dollars each year.

Maya Pedal

designer:
   Asociación Maya Pedal
other partners/clients/producers:
   Pedal Energy Development
   Alternatives (PEDAL)
geographical implementation/
market/availability:
   Guatemala
status:
   Project implemented
website:
   www.mayapedal.org

Bicycles are one of the most common and accessible forms of transportation in the developing world. Maya Pedal, an NGO based in San Andrés Itzapa, Guatemala, recycles bicycles and builds pedal-powered machines, called bicimáquinas, to support and catalyze small-scale, sustainable local enterprises and businesses. The machines serve as tools for development, efficiency, economic productivity, and even public health.

The project has developed economical original designs for machines that it continues to replicate. The current diverse model and prototype offerings are a blender, water pump, tricycle and trailer, coffeemaker, corn degrainer, metal sharpener, microconcrete vibrator for masonry, washing machine, generator, soil plow, nut sheller, and wood saw. Each of the devices is powered by human pedaling, a form of renewable energy, using a bike's gears and pedal system, which are reworked and attached to the tools.

The Asociación Campesino in San Andrés Itzapa, for example, uses a bicycle corn degrainer to produce animal feed and a bicycle blender to make shampoo. The Family Group Pachay las Lomas in San Martín uses a bicycle water pump to tap a clean aquifer 98 feet (30 m) underground and runs a workshop to teach masons how to lay tiles using the microconcrete vibrator. The bicimáquinas are designed to act as intermediate technologies to help individuals, families, and groups work toward greater production capacities in agricultural or other small businesses. All the machines are built individually by Maya Pedal from old bicycle parts and supplementary material such as concrete, wood, or metal.

Maya Pedal shares its machine designs with other nonprofits and NGOs that do community-based work, contributing to open-source design collaboration. It also provides training workshops to groups interested in pedal technology on subjects including bike repair and maintenance and development of new uses for the existing machine technologies. In addition, Maya Pedal partners with local programs and organizations in Guatemala to help promote the use of repaired bicycles as modes of transportation.

Maya Pedal integrates do-it-yourself ingenuity with a worthwhile enterprise that supports both its producers and its customers through access to tools, capital, and jobs. The programs successfully reuse bicycles, commercialize bike machines, expand the efficiency and capacities of existing businesses, and invest in the environmental and social sustainability of communities in the developing world. Maya Pedal was founded in 1997 in collaboration with Canadian group PEDAL and became an official Guatemalan development organization in 2001.

El Proyecto Paraguas

In 2002 Argentina underwent a massive social, economic, and political upheaval that left many small businesses bankrupt. Argentine architect Gustavo Crembil, along with Peter Lynch, Crembil's current partner at New York–based Studio THEM, and Diego Dragotto and Pablo Capitanelli, then partners at Quinoa Arquitectura, saw an opportunity to create a small business that would make and sell baskets by combining work already being done by two very different groups, one rural and one urban. Each group relied on small-scale ingenuity and enterprise, so the designers combined their efforts into a collaborative force that would share resources for mutual benefit to both groups and the surrounding community.

The urban component, Cirugía Urbana ("Urban Surgery"), was an informal group of people who scavenged the street for material to use and sell. EnTrama(r), on the other hand, was a group of rural basket weavers (*entramar* means "to build the framework for"). In Crembil's plan, discarded plastic water bottles, collected by the Cirugía Urbana scavengers, would be sold to the weavers as raw material for their baskets. The EnTrama(r) workers would then slice the bottles into long strips using a rotational cutting tool specially designed by Crembil and his partners. The weavers would benefit from increased efficiency and a sustainable supply of material, while the scavengers would have a steady distribution chain for their goods. Simultaneously, the weavers would provide hands-on training to the scavengers in the craft of basket weaving, allowing the urban workers to personally add value to their found materials.

With the agreement in place, Urban Surgery and EnTrama(r) became El Proyecto Paraguas, or "The Umbrella Project," a symbiotic partnership between the rural and urban, design and manufacturing, communities and individuals. "The aim of the 'umbrella' is to bring together the two disenfranchised economies and cultures (urban and rural) for them to share technologies, knowledge, skills, and resources and build more economical and political leverage," explains Crembil. "They even started to talk about unionizing the informal garbage collection."

The small-scale design enterprise is an example of what the developers call a social technology project—one that lends greater efficiency and distribution potential to craft-based economies. "The technology is an excuse to build other political skills such as leadership, consensus, and so on," states Crembil.

designer:
Gustavo Crembil
other partners/clients/producers:
Pablo Capitanelli, Diego Dragotto, Peter Lynch, local manufacturers
geographical implementation/ market/availability:
Argentina
status:
Project implemented
website:
www.studiothem.com

Publicolor

Publicolor uses the power of color and collaboration to transform struggling public schools into invigorating learning environments. Through the program that was founded by industrial designer Ruth Lande Shuman in 1996, painting and design become the backbone of youth development programs that help at-risk students become more engaged citizens. Students, along with Publicolor volunteers, paint the public spaces of their dreary schools, transforming them into inviting and visually stimulating learning environments. Through participation in the painting and supplementary programs, which include weekly career workshops, one-on-one tutoring sessions, and community service projects, Publicolor students are empowered to enrich their schools, their neighborhoods, and themselves. To date, Publicolor has transformed 105 public schools and 115 community facilities including health clinics, community centers, homeless shelters, and police precincts. Well over 300,000 teachers and students

now work in colorful, interesting environments where the importance of education has been underscored by the power of design.

Through a creative approach anchored in high expectations of its participants, the program teaches students the marketable skill of commercial painting, as well as strong work habits, effective social tools, and practical, transferable academic lessons. Publicolor students have significantly better high school and college graduation rates than their classmates, while the schools and community facilities renovated by the program report increased morale, higher productivity, a new sense of community, and a far greater sense of safety. "Now I am doing better in school," says 13-year-old Publicolor student Vincheskia W. "If we messed up painting, we had to do it over. Now while I am doing my homework and I mess up, I do it over."

Currently Publicolor works in the five boroughs of New York City and is beginning to replicate its programs

in Pittsburgh's public schools. The program has transformed environments and lives through design, breaking the cycle of poverty, empowering students, and changing the expectations of school administrators and parents. "In struggling schools, the environment is often one of low expectations and incompletion," states Shuman. "When we complete a transformation there is always a sense of accomplishment and success, which hopefully will lead to future successes."

designer:
Ruth Lande Shuman
other partners/clients/producers:
New York City public schools,
various community organizations
**geographical implementation/
market/availability:**
New York City
status:
Project implemented
website:
www.publicolor.org

Sweat Equity Enterprises (SEE)

designers:
Damon Butler, Nell Daniel,
Marc Ecko
other partners/clients/producers:
Marc Ecko Enterprises, New Era,
RadioShack, Saks Fifth Avenue,
Skechers, Zoo York, and others
**geographical implementation/
market/availability:**
USA
status:
Project implemented
website:
www.sweatequityenterprises.org

Founded in 2004 in New York City, SEE is a design-based learning program that allows young people to work with and for innovative retail companies. Through partnerships between teenagers and businesses such as Marc Ecko Enterprises, Skechers, and others, youth and industry form an innovation lab that develops shoes, sportswear, consumer packaging, graphic design, marketing campaigns, and more. SEE currently partners with four alternative high schools around the country and has plans to expand into new cities. Students are selected by application based on their interest in design and commitment to the rigorous program.

Participants are given an opportunity to analyze and reconceptualize products from an inside perspective, then develop and propose their own professional designs for industry partners. Any proceeds from the designs or contributions go toward college scholarships for the students and support for the SEE program. Concepts prototyped have included shoes for Skechers, watches for Timex, skateboards for Zoo York, outerwear for Marc Ecko, and graphic design for New York Cares, with upcoming projects including cars for Nissan and electronics for RadioShack.

SEE provides young people with access to collaborative work in a professional environment and teaches a variety of skills: creative (project and information management, marketing, design fundamentals, computer-aided design programs), socioeconomic (conflict resolution, financial management, problem solving), and academic (research, math, social sciences, critical thinking). A division of the program also integrates the work into the school's design curriculum.

SEE is more than an after-school opportunity for teenagers; it has given the participating companies new perspectives on marketing and product development, since most of them target a youthful market. This engages both the participants, who are simultaneously co-designers and the desired consumers, and the corporate partners, who rely on the students for design ideas and feedback, while they also cultivate a talented creative workforce.

Uganda Stove Manufacturers, Ltd. (UGASTOVE)

UGASTOVE is an African enterprise success story, exemplifying what strategic investment, social entrepreneurship, and open-source, need-based design can enable. Based in Kampala, Uganda, the NGO develops and builds affordable, clean stoves for residential and commercial use and relies on local labor, resources, and research to create regional franchise opportunities. The group, formerly known as Urban Community Development Agencies (UCODEA), has been in operation for more than 20 years, employing 55 workers in multiple dealer outlets and fabrication facilities. In that time, it has distributed more than 20,000 charcoal, rocket wood, institutional, and custom stoves across Uganda. Through these production projects, UGASTOVE innovatively engages the urban poor, stimulates socioeconomic development, and makes a commitment to environmental health and improved living standards. The stoves are affordable and burn cleaner than alternatives, offering more efficient combustion and

a reduction of emissions, which allows UGASTOVE to qualify for carbon credits. The appliances are constructed of durable sheet-metal casings in the organization's signature colors of orange and red, and are lined with ceramic for optimal heat retention.

In addition to making stoves, UGASTOVE engages in international research forums on environmental sustainability, climate control, and improved stove-science research, and offers training and franchise opportunities for new enterprise growth. The NGO also provides services including garbage collection for households in and around Kampala and supports a women's network engaged in producing retained-heat cookers and other income-generating opportunities.

What began as a community-based organization in Kampala has grown since 2002 into a thriving social enterprise under the leadership of Kawere Mohammad, director of UGASTOVE and second-generation stove builder. UGASTOVE receives ongoing support from African and inter-

national NGOs and foundations, the US Environmental Protection Agency, and the Public-Private Partnerships for Urban Environment, a government group funded by the United Nations Development Program. UGASTOVE serves as a case study for viable social entrepreneurship where it is most needed.

partners/clients/producers:
Aprovecho, Center for
Entrepreneurship in International
Health and Development,
ClimateCare, Partnership for
Clean Indoor Air
**geographical implementation/
market/availability:**
Uganda
status:
Limited distribution
website:
www.ucodea.com

cknowled ments

Too many people to name have contributed, knowingly or unknowingly, to the realization of this book and to my optimism and perseverance while writing it. To mention a few: special thanks to my parents, George and Anna Pilloton, my unyielding cheerleaders, for instilling entrepreneurial and humanitarian values, for lending their dining room to Project H as its first office, and for making it clear why people always thank their parents first; to my sisters and BFFs, Molly and Maggie, for never-ending silliness and "sistertary" skills; to Miller, my biggest fan and critic, for sanity by osmosis and coffee every morning; and to two Pings and two Fas for being my shepherds in absentia.

To everyone who actively contributed to the words, images, editing, design, and publication of this book, thank you for giving me an opportunity to be heard and for your expertise and critique: Diana Murphy for approaching me in May 2008, believing in a 26-year-old's naively optimistic ideas and remaining a friend throughout the intense publishing process; Scott Stowell and Serifcan Ozcan at Open for their art, humor, and uncanny ability to make information beautiful and unignorable; Allan Chochinov for a provocative foreword and for publishing a manifesto that arguably put this whole book in motion; Meghan Conaton for thousands of Microsoft Word comments and catching my sloppy mistakes; Susan Szenasy for believing in Project H when it was nothing more than a brainchild dreamt about over coffee; and everyone at Metropolis Books and D.A.P.

Thanks to a troupe of Project H partners and designers: directors Paul Donald, Laura Galloway, Sarah Rich, and Emily Ritter, the original "chica loca," whose friendship dates back to 1997 in Cuernavaca; Ryan Duke, Kim Karlsrud, and all the Project H chapter heads worldwide; Heleen De Goey, Project H's first intern; Dan Grossman; Kristina Drury; Neha Thatte; Ilona de Jongh; Grant Gibbs and Cynthia Koenig from Hippo Water Roller; Heather Fleming and Paul Dreyer from Engineers Without Borders; Haath Mein Sehat; Jackson Kaguri; Rob and Carol Auld; the teachers of the Kutamba AIDS Orphans School in Uganda; Laura Brandmeier and the amazing team of students from Pratt Institute's Design Management Program; Ideablob; and every Project H donor, supporter, and friend.

And thank you to each person who, in a moment of encouragement, argument, or unintentional serendipity, helped me get to something great: Cameron Sinclair and Kate Stohr, mentors, landlords, and matchmakers; Alex Steffen for inspiration over Indian food and a particularly lovely e-mail on August 2, 2008; Valerie Casey for partnership and ambition in the Year of the Ox; Rob Davis for pushing me to make up my own rules; Joe Gebbia; Sayuri Stabrowski; Sara Dinoto; the creators of *Arrested Development*; Jill Fehrenbacher; Abigail Doan; Jeanne Montague and Chad Overway; Dave and Sandy Asheim; Jared Cooper; Muffin; Gus; Beatrix Kiddo; Nicholas Okuley; the School of the Art Institute of Chicago; Ben Nicholson; Wesley Honstein for his chocolate chip cookie recipe; and a certain chair of a certain department at a certain design school for giving me someone to prove wrong. And to the best teachers I've ever had: Robert McAnulty, Anders Nereim, Helen Maria Nugent, Mitch Cohen, David Goldman, Kathy Jablonski, and Tayeko Kaufman.

Lastly, thanks to all who contributed their projects, work, stories, and material to these pages. I apologize if any information is incorrect or out-of-date, or if I have neglected to accurately give credit where credit is due. I have made every attempt to correctly identify and acknowledge the sources, authors, and owners of all work and visual content.
Emily Pilloton

credits

contents

Project H Design: 5 (foreword, acknowledgments)

Design Can Change the World

Courtesy Appropriate Infrastructure Development Group (AIDG): 42; Aresa Biodetection: 45; The Australian National University: 33; Larissa Co: 41; danone.communities, Thomas Haley, Sipa Press: 26; fuseproject: 21; Alexandre Grau: 11; Mike Grote: 24; Amelia Hart: 12; International Development Enterprises (IDE): 17; Mark Kelley: 18; Kennedy & Violich Architecture, Ltd.: 36, 37; KickStart International: 27; Matthew Miller: 34; Emily Pilloton: 16; Project H Design: 39; Publicolor: 23

water

Air2Water: 50; The Australian National University: 58, 60, 61; D-Lab at the Massachusetts Institute of Technology (MIT): 74, 75; Department of Water and Sanitation in Developing Countries (Sandec) at the Swiss Federal Institute of Aquatic Science and Technology (Eawag): 85; DPM Water Technologies, Ltd.: 52, 53; Electrolux: 51; Environmental Designworks, LLC: 83; FilterForGood.com: 56, 57; Hippo Water Roller: 66, 68, 69; Frank Husson, Solar Solutions Laboratories: 55; IDEO: 54; John TODD ECOLOGICAL Design, Inc.: 62, 63; LIFESAVER Systems: 71; Chris Lovin: 78, 79; Matthew Miller: 77; Resource Development International–Cambodia (RDIC)/Ideas at Work: 80, 81; © Sancor Industries, Ltd.: 64, 65; Vestergaard Frandsen: 72, 73

well-being

Adaptive Eyecare: 88, 89; Allen-Vanguard CORP: 108, 109; DAC Research Center: 112; Freedom HIV/AIDS: 94, 95; fuseproject: 105; The Home Depot: 96, 97; IDEO: 116, 117; Jaipur Foot, Bhagwan Mahaveer Viklang Sahayata Samiti (BMVSS): 100, 101; © LifeScan, Inc.: 106, 107; Hân Pham: 91; PhotoGenesis Medical: 92, 93; Pyng Medical: 103; RedStart Design, LLC: 113; Mark Serr: 99; StarSight International, Ltd.: 110, 111; © 2008 Target Pharmacy bottle, Target Pharmacy and the Bullseye Design are trademarks of Target Brands, Inc. The Target Pharmacy bottle system is covered by the following U.S. patents: 7,311,205; 7,413,082; D542,611; D572,593; D581,275. Other U.S. and international patents pending: 114, 115

energy

Courtesy Appropriate Infrastructure Development Group (AIDG): 146, 147; Better Energy Systems, Ltd.: 144, 145; Brunton: 142, 143; Teresita B. Cochran, Sustainably Minded Interactive Technology (SMIT): 136 bottom, 137; Freeplay Energy: 149; Andy Hammons: 131 top; Devin Henry 2008: 128; Chia-Ying Lee: 151; Matt Meshulam: 132; Malcolm Meyer: 131 bottom; Mixer Group: 150; Motion 2 Energy Power, Inc. (M2E): 141; Patricia Murray, Durham Skywriter: 129; Marc Nolte: 125 bottom; Stephanie Poon: 138, 139; Rich, Brilliant, Willing: 134; Southwest Windpower: 120, 121; Lizzie Spraggs: 127; Matthew Strom: 133; Sustainable Dance Club (SDC): 125 top; Lotte van Stekelburg: 124; Sven Wiederholt: 122, 123

education

Anders Sune Berg, Bosch & Fjord: 177; Mark Champkins: 183; Eddie Chiu: 165; Design that Matters: 158, 159; Don't Lean Back, Ltd. (DLB): 163; Enabling Devices: 157; fuseproject: 172–75; Amelia Hart: 167–69; IDEO: 178; Dean Kober, Marko Pavlovic: 171 bottom; © 2009 Modality, Inc.: 154; Emily Pilloton: 181; Project H Design: 160; Elvir Tabakovic, Marko Pavlovic: 171 top row; Treeblocks: 182

mobility

Bill Albrecht: 197; Ralph Baleno: 198; Calfee Design: 192, 193; Jin Woo Han: 206, 207; Chris Howard: 211; Institute for Affordable Transportation (IAT): 188; Johnson Outdoors's Eureka! Tents: 201; Ed Lucero: 194; Steven McBride: 204; Herman van Ommen, Arnhem: 191; © SkySails GmbH & Co. KG: 202, 203; Ultra Motor: 186, 187; Walk Score: 208; Zipcar, Inc.: 213

food

Courtesy Appropriate Infrastructure Development Group (AIDG): 218, 219; BCK: 220, 221; Compatible Technology International (CTI): 222; Daily Dump: 225; Kristina Drury: 236, 237; NatureMill, Inc.: 230, 231; Nutriset: 234; OXO: 232, 233; Jennifer Panepinto: 228, 229; Julie Pudlowski: 235; Mark Serr: 216, 217; StoveTec/Aprovecho Research Center: 226, 227; Y Water: 238, 239

play

Ben Arent: 256, 257; Jonathan Barth: 270; Bubbles Visuals/Anke Adriaans: 243; Amy Franceschini: 250, 251; © Giantmicrobes, Inc.: 252, 253; Peter Henkes, Kidsonroof: 258, 259; Eric Hersman: 246; Horizon Fuel Cell Technologies: 254, 255; © Imagekontainer/Inga Knoelke: 245; Rolf Küng: 248, 249; © 2009 The LEGO Group: 260, 261; © NIKE, Inc.: 262, 263; Parsons the New School for Design: 247; Playful Invention Company, Inc. (PICO): 266, 267; Sony Corp.: 265; Herbert Wiggerman: 268

enterprise

Artecnica: 276, 277; © Bank of America: 288; Martin Barnard: 275 bottom; Bill Clyne: 280; Joe Cogan: 275 top; Gustavo Crembil: 293; danone.communities, Thomas Haley, Sipa Press: 287; © Futurelab 2008: 285; James Gambrione: 283; Michael Gillman, www.michaelgillman.com: 290, 291; IDEO: 289; Matthew Miller: 299; Rich Miller, Denver's Road Home, rabble + rouser, OZ Architecture: 279; Publicolor: 295; Sweat Equity Enterprises (SEE): 296; WFP Photolibrary: 282

page 303
Design Revolution
credits

**Library of Congress
Cataloging-in-Publication Data**

Pilloton, Emily.
Design revolution:
100 products that empower people/
Emily Pilloton;
foreword by Allan Chochinov.
--1st ed.
p. cm.
ISBN 978-1-933045-95-5
1. Design, Industrial.
I. Title.
II. Title: 100 products that
empower people.
TS171.4.P55 2009
745.2--dc22
2009011291

Project director:
   Diana Murphy
Design and production:
   Open
   www.notclosed.com
Separations and printing:
   Asia Pacific Offset, Inc., China

Set in Graphik by Christian Schwartz
and printed on Thai wood-free paper

**METROPOLIS
BOOKS**

Metropolis Books is a joint
publishing program of:

**D.A.P./
Distributed Art Publishers, Inc.**
155 Sixth Avenue, 2nd floor
New York NY 10013
tel 212 627 1999
fax 212 627 9484
www.artbook.com

and

Metropolis Magazine
61 West 23rd Street, 4th floor
New York NY 10010
tel 212 627 9977
fax 212 627 9988
www.metropolismag.com

Available through D.A.P./
Distributed Art Publishers, Inc.,
New York.

Proceeds from the sale
of this book will support the work
of Project H Design.